Question and Answer Encyclopedia

The USA

Question
and Answer
Encyclopedia

The USA

p

This is a Parragon Publishing Book
This edition published in 2002

Parragon Publishing
Queen Street House
4 Queen Street
Bath BA1 1HE, UK

ISBN 0-75258-059-0

Printed in China

Produced by
Monkey Puzzle Media Ltd

Written by Nicola Barber, Jason Hook, Patricia Levy,
Chris Oxlade, and Sean Sheehan
Illustrated by Adam Hook, David McAllister, and Mike White
Edited by Linda Sonntag
Designed by Sarah Crouch, Tim Mayer, and Victoria Webb
Artwork commissioning: Roger Goddard-Coote
Project manager: Alex Edmonds

Contents

The 50 States

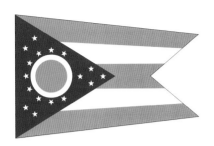

ALASKA

CANADA

PACIFIC OCEAN

The United States

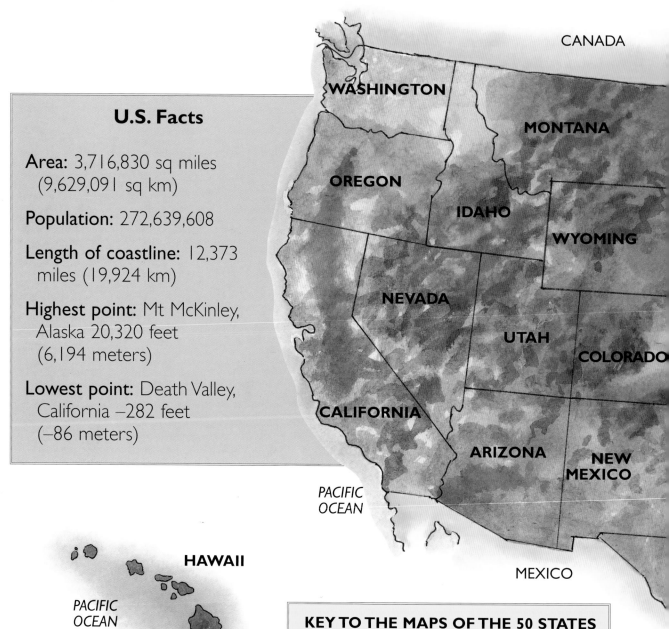

CANADA

WASHINGTON

MONTANA

OREGON

IDAHO

WYOMING

NEVADA

UTAH

COLORADO

CALIFORNIA

ARIZONA

NEW MEXICO

PACIFIC OCEAN

MEXICO

U.S. Facts

Area: 3,716,830 sq miles (9,629,091 sq km)

Population: 272,639,608

Length of coastline: 12,373 miles (19,924 km)

Highest point: Mt McKinley, Alaska 20,320 feet (6,194 meters)

Lowest point: Death Valley, California −282 feet (−86 meters)

HAWAII

PACIFIC OCEAN

Hawaii and Alaska are not shown at the same scale as the rest of the U.S.

KEY TO THE MAPS OF THE 50 STATES

☐ **National capital (Washington, D.C.)**

■ **State capitals**

● **Other main cities**

Capital Facts

Area of District of Columbia:
67 sq miles (173.5 sq km)

Population: Washington 607,000
Residential area 5,689,263

The Capitol building and the Washington
Monument in Washington, D.C.

NORTH DAKOTA

MINNESOTA

SOUTH DAKOTA

NEBRASKA

IOWA

WISCONSIN

MICHIGAN

NEW HAMPSHIRE

VERMONT

MAINE

NEW YORK

MASSACHUSETTS

RHODE ISLAND

PENNSYLVANIA

CONNECTICUT

NEW JERSEY

OHIO

INDIANA

ILLINOIS

WEST VIRGINIA

DELAWARE

MARYLAND

WASHINGTON, D.C.

VIRGINIA

KANSAS

MISSOURI

KENTUCKY

NORTH CAROLINA

TENNESSEE

OKLAHOMA

ARKANSAS

SOUTH CAROLINA

GEORGIA

ATLANTIC OCEAN

TEXAS

ALABAMA

MISSISSIPPI

FLORIDA

LOUISIANA

GULF OF MEXICO

What lay dormant for 130 years before waking up in 1980?

THE ALREADY GRUMBLING VOLCANO MOUNT ST HELENS. ON MAY 18, 1980 this peak in the Cascade mountains in Washington erupted when a severe earthquake opened a crack along its side. The side of the mountain blew out and debris, lava, and ash spread out in a 17 mile (27 km) arc, flattening forests in its path. Thirty people were killed and the height of the mountain 8,229 ft (2,508 m) was reduced by 1,312 ft (400 m).

How did the first families to cross the continent meet a disastrous end?

Marcus Whitman, his wife Narcissa, the Rev. Henry Spalding, and his wife made the first wagon train crossing that included women. They built a mission at Waillatpu, and helped other families make the crossing after them. But in 1874 they and 12 other people were killed by Native Americans.

Where can you see a phantom ship sailing across a volcano?

In Crater Lake National Park, southwestern Oregon. A lake has formed in the crater of an extinct volcano. The lake is surrounded by cliffs 500—2,000 ft (150—600 m) high. At the southern end is a mass of lava, which looks like a ship under sail.

Who were the first Europeans to sight Oregon?

Probably Spanish sailors in the 1500s. The headland of the Columbia River was given the name Cape Disappointment because explorers could not find the river mouth. In 1792 it was discovered by Robert Gray who named it after his ship, the *Columbia*.

Where does a snake run into hell?

The Snake River runs through Idaho. It cuts through the Rocky Mountains in the west of the United States at Hell's Canyon. This is the deepest gorge in North America at 7,776 ft (2,370 m). It is part of the Hell's Canyon Wilderness, a National Park.

Crater Lake is the second deepest lake in North America.

Washington

Oregon

Idaho

Which is the apple state?

The area of Washington to the west of the Cascade mountain range has some of the thickest forests in the world. It is also one of the wettest areas in the U.S., and this makes the area good for growing produce. In fact, Washington grows more apples than any other state in the United States. East of the Cascade Range there is little rain and few trees.

Why did Lewis and Clarke go up-river?

Lewis and Clarke were the two men chosen by President Thomas Jefferson in 1804 to explore the land west of the Mississippi. They took a small party and followed the Missouri River to its source, crossed the continental divide and then found and followed the Columbia River. Their expedition gave America its claim to the Oregon territories.

How did Idaho get its unusual shape?

Oⁿ THE MAP IDAHO IS SHAPED LIKE A PLATFORM BOOT WITH A large, almost square section in the south but an odd north-south section. Idaho was created after the six states and one Canadian province that surround it had created their borders. It is a strip of land that no one else claimed. The surrounding settlers would have acted differently, had they realized what a wealth of silver, zinc, lead, and lumber Idaho would eventually give up!

Where can you see salmon climbing a ladder?

The Columbia River in Washington has been dammed in several places and this makes it impossible for salmon to reach their breeding grounds. So at Bonneville Dam a special ladder has been built where the salmon can jump in stages up the height of the dam.

Which Seattle-born businessman is mega-rich?

Bill Gates of the Microsoft Corporation. He made his first billion at the age of 31 after inventing the MS-DOS system and then Windows. Today he is one of the richest men in the world.

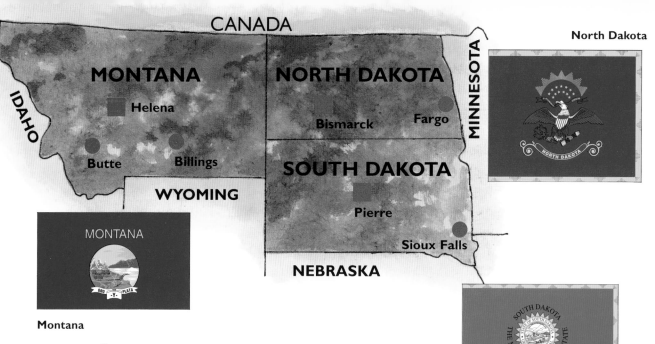

CANADA

MONTANA

Helena

IDAHO

Butte   Billings

WYOMING

NORTH DAKOTA

Bismarck   Fargo

MINNESOTA

SOUTH DAKOTA

Pierre

Sioux Falls

NEBRASKA

North Dakota

MONTANA
ORO ·Y· PLATA

Montana

South Dakota

Why is Montana named the Bonanza State?

Montana has many nicknames, including Big Sky Country,
Land of the Shining Mountains, and the Treasure State. It's
called Bonanza because of its wealth of natural resources.
Montana has huge stretches of fertile soil suitable for wheat
and grassland for grazing. It has valuable minerals and
millions of acres of timber, particularly spruce, larch, and
pine, all fast-growing and very good for commercial use.
Another major resource is its beautiful scenery, which
attracts thousands of tourists each year.

What was Custer's Last Stand?

In 1874 gold prospectors flooded
into South Dakota regardless of
the understandably hostile Sioux
whose land it was. General Custer
was part of the force sent to
protect the prospectors. In 1876,
disobeying orders, he led his
troops into an ambush by 6,000
Native Americans at Little Bighorn.
He and all 200 of his soldiers were
killed. This event was named
Custer's Last Stand.

What are the Badlands?

An area of North and South
Dakota where erosion has carved
strange shapes out of the rock and
there is no vegetation. Pioneers
named it the Badlands because it
was so difficult to cross. In places,
underground lignite (brown coal)
fires have melted the rock and
created a mass of striking
colors. The remains of
saber-toothed tigers have
been found there.

To the east of Montana, the Great
Plains stretch for miles; to the west
the Rockies tower over the land.

Who was Calamity Jane?

Martha Jane Canary, born 1852. She lived in Virginia City and was a very good horsewoman. She drove freight wagons for a time and then went to Deadwood in South Dakota during the gold rush of 1864. Many stories tell of her exploits, including how she fought Native Americans, wore men's clothes, and got very drunk.

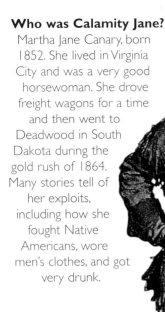

Calamity Jane was born in Princeton, Missouri. She is said to have promised "calamity" to any man who tried to court her… but in 1885 she got married!

Where can you find the second longest mountain chain in the world?

The Rocky Mountains, Montana. They begin far north of Montana in Alaska, cross Canada, and dominate the western third of the United States, but their main bulk is in Montana. Granite Peak is the highest mountain in the state at 12,799 ft (3,840 m).

Where is "the richest hill on Earth"?

At Butte, Montana. In 1881 a prospector, Marcus Daly, who was searching for silver, found copper instead. The town of Butte grew up quickly and soon turned into a lawless place with bandits controlling the roads. Daly's Anaconda Company became one of the biggest mining companies in the world.

Why is "big" an important word for Alaska?

WHEN ALASKA JOINED THE UNION IT INCREASED THE size of the U.S. by a fifth. It brought with it some big facts. It has 28,000 miles (44,800 km) of glaciers; the highest mountain in North America (Mount McKinley); the largest carnivorous land mammal (the kodiac bear); and part of the longest navigable waterway in the world (the Yukon River).

Where would you find the world's tallest manmade structure?

Surprisingly, not in New York City but in North Dakota where the KTHI-TV mast is 2,063 ft (619 m) high. It is supported by guy wires and would not stand up on its own. For the tallest self-supporting structure, you would have to go to Toronto in Canada.

Alaska

Pacific Ocean

John Wayne is possibly the most famous cowboy-actor in the world.

Who added his own bad name to the English language?

In 1950 Joseph McCarthy, the senator for Wisconsin, claimed he had a list of communists employed by the State Department. The Senate Committee for un-American activities began investigations into communist activity within government. Many people in the film industry were ruined by the investigations, although no accusations were ever proved. Finally McCarthy went too far and accused President Eisenhower of being a communist. The word "McCarthyism" now means the persecution of innocent people with unproved charges.

How does Minnesota take care of its wildlife?

Minnesota has vast resources of forest and was once a major logging center. Recently, Minnesota has set aside more land for wildlife preservation than any other state. In several areas where trees were cut down, the forest has been replanted.

Who created the famous cartoon Peanuts?

Charles M. Schultz. He was born in Minneapolis, Minnesota, in 1922 and invented the cartoon strip Peanuts in 1950. It was originally named Li'l Folks, but has always included the beagle dog Snoopy and his owner Charlie Brown. It is the most successful cartoon strip in the world.

Which is America's cheesiest state?

Wisconsin has been America's leading producer of milk since 1920, and today has about 1,750,000 cows. The first cheese factory was opened there in 1864 and Wisconsin cheese is internationally renowned. The state also has many creameries and butter factories.

Why did Marian Morrison change names?

Marian BECAME ONE OF IOWA'S MOST FAMOUS CITIZENS, starring in films such as *Stagecoach* (1939), *True Grit* (1969), *The Alamo* (1960) and many more. He was in fact John Wayne, born in Winterset, Iowa, in 1907. He changed his name, for obvious reasons, in the 1930s.

How did wheat from Iowa make bread in Moscow?

IOWA PRODUCES MASSES OF GRAIN—OVER A BILLION TONS IN SOME YEARS. IN THE 1950s the rest of the U.S. bought little of this harvest and Iowa farmers began to suffer. Then Soviet premier Kruschev visited Iowa and set up a trade link between Iowa and Russia. The trade earned the state a huge annual revenue and it came to depend on it. In 1979 there was a trade embargo (ban) following the Afghanistan war, but the link was re-established in 1981.

How did a Gumm become a Garland?

Filmstar Judy Garland (1922—69) was born in Grand Rapids, Minnesota, although she didn't spend much of her time there. Her real name was Frances Gumm and she worked as a child performer in her parents' singing act before being spotted by Louis B. Mayer of MGM studios.

Where is the birthplace of the artist formerly known as Prince?

Prince Rogers Nelson was born in Minneapolis on June 7th 1959. By the age of 12 he was playing in a band. He went on to produce songs such as *Purple Rain*, and the soundtrack to *Batman*. In 1993 he changed his name to a symbol made up of the two biological signs for male and female.

How do people enjoy Wisconsin's great outdoors?

Hunting is the most popular sporting activity in Wisconsin—for bear, game birds, and deer. The vast areas of lakeland offer fishing —especially for the curiously named muskellunge—and watersports of many kinds. In winter there are iceboat races on Lake Winnebago.

CANADA

Lake Superior

N. DAKOTA

Duluth

MICHIGAN

MINNESOTA

St Paul

S. DAKOTA

Minneapolis

WISCONSIN

Lake Michigan

Madison

Milwaukee

NEBRASKA

IOWA

ILLINOIS

OHIO

Des Moines

MISSOURI

WISCONSIN

1848

Wisconsin

IOWA

Iowa

Minnesota

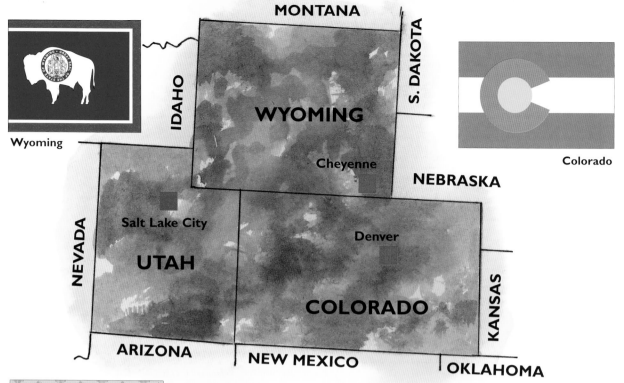

MONTANA

WYOMING

IDAHO

S. DAKOTA

Cheyenne

NEBRASKA

NEVADA

UTAH

Salt Lake City

Denver

COLORADO

KANSAS

ARIZONA

NEW MEXICO

OKLAHOMA

Wyoming

Colorado

Utah

What is the Devil's Tower?

Sixty million years ago in northeastern Wyoming, molten lava forced its way up through sandstone rock and gradually cooled. Over the millennia the sandstone was eroded until all that remained was the Devil's Tower—a fluted column of volcanic rock standing 865 ft (260 m) high above the trees.

Which religious group founded Utah?

In 1847 Utah was Native American land. Then a religious group named the Mormons, persecuted in the East because the men of the sect took several wives, settled near Salt Lake and founded the state. Their leader, Brigham Young, became governor of the state. Even today, more than 70 percent of the people living in Utah are Mormons.

Arches National Park

What is the Rainbow Bridge?

THE RAINBOW BRIDGE IS THE WORLD'S LARGEST NATURAL BRIDGE, FOUND in a national park in southeastern Utah. It is a salmon pink sandstone arch 309 ft (93 m) high and 278 ft (84 m) wide. Native Americans once considered it a sacred site. The first white men saw it in 1909.

Where can you sit on the Great White Throne?

In Southern Utah the Virgin River has formed a canyon between huge sheer-walled sandstone cliffs. A Mormon scout was the first white man to discover the place in 1858. Set into the east wall inside the canyon is a natural structure that looks like a massive chair, and is named the Great White Throne. The area is very beautiful and is now a national park.

Which Wild West state first gave women the vote?

Wyoming is famous for its Wild West stories of cattle ranchers and wagon trains. Its pioneers were fur traders who fought the Native Americans and took their territory. One of Wyoming's best known frontiersmen was Buffalo Bill Cody, who founded the town of Cody. Wyoming is named the Equality State, because in 1869 it was the first state to give women the vote and to allow them to stand for public office. The first woman governor in the United States was Nellie Taloe Ross, elected in Wyoming in 1929.

What do Esther, Spotted Tail, Robert and John have in common?

They are all famous citizens of Wyoming, Utah, and California. Wyoming's Esther Morris was an important figure in the women's suffrage movement—in 1870 she became the first American woman to be made a justice of the peace. Spotted Tail was a Wyoming Sioux chief who for a long time preserved his nation's territory and avoided war with white men. Among Utah's famous are Robert Redford, born in California but now living in a Utah ski resort. Colorado was home to John Denver, the singer and songwriter known for songs such as *Windsong* and *Leaving on a Jet Plane*.

Which was the world's first national park?

YELLOWSTONE NATIONAL PARK, STRETCHING ACROSS WYOMING, Idaho, and Montana, was established in 1872. It was the first protected area for wildlife in the world. Here you can see the geyser named Old Faithful, the hot springs, the Yellowstone Falls, rock formations, and herds of wild buffalo.

Where can you find a palace inside a cliff?

At Mesa Verde, Colorado, which has the best preserved cliff dwellings in America. The steep hill is riddled with more than 600 cave dwellings. One of these is known as the Cliff Palace and has 223 rooms. The cliff was inhabited from early Christian times.

Which is the highest city in the U.S.?

Denver, the capital city of Colorado. Denver is the gateway to the Rocky Mountains, which dominate the western half of the state. It calls itself the "Mile High City." Eight hundred of Colorado's mountains are above 14,223 ft (4,334 m) high.

Where is the lowest point in the western hemisphere?

Straddling the border between California and Nevada is Death Valley. It is a deep trough between two mountain ranges and 550 sq miles (330 sq km) of it lie 286 ft (86 m) below sea level. It is the lowest, and also the hottest, place in the western hemisphere.

Which U.S. state produces the most gold?

Since the Comstock Lode was discovered in 1859 Nevada has been a major producer of both gold and silver. The lode ran out after about 20 years but many smaller deposits have since been found. Today, mining for gold, silver, barite, mercury, lithium, and gemstones is one of Nevada's most important industries.

Which state has the grisliest criminal record?

California has the largest prison population of the U.S. with 153,010 inmates, the highest number of murders (2,916 in 1996), and the most prisoners (both men and women) on death row (454 in 1996). Incidentally, the U.S. has the largest prison population in the world.

Where can you find the largest and tallest living thing on Earth?

California

IN CALIFORNIA, OF COURSE.

The General Sherman giant sequoia tree in Sequoia National Park is 280 ft (85 m) high and weighs an estimated 2,461 tons.

General Sherman
Giant Sequoia

Which state is the top of the pops?

Ever since California was admitted to the union in 1850, it has had the highest population growth rate of the U.S. In the beginning, it had a population of 10,000. By 1940, less than a century later, its population was 7 million! By 1970, California had more people than any other state in the U.S., and it has remained the most populated ever since. Los Angeles County alone has more citizens than at least 40 of the other states! Nowadays the population of California stands at just under 30 million.

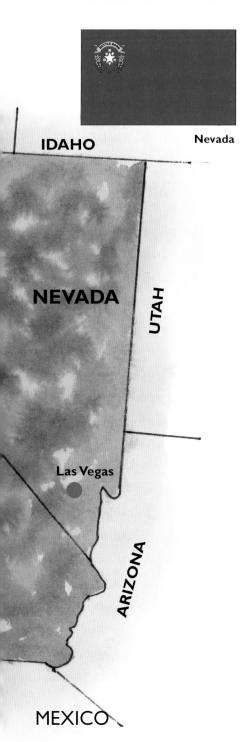

IDAHO

Nevada

NEVADA

UTAH

Las Vegas

ARIZONA

MEXICO

San Francisco's Golden Gate Bridge was built in 1937.

What is Methuselah doing in Nevada?

Methuselah is the pet name of a giant bristlecone pine tree growing on Wheeler Peak, Nevada. It is thought to be the oldest living tree in America at around 4,900 years old.

What sort of chips can you find in Santa Clara?

In the 1970s and 1980s a large number of electronics companies settled in the Santa Clara Valley, an area southwest of San Francisco. It later became known as Silicon Valley after the material that computer chips are made of.

Where can you visit a prison in a park?

At the Golden Gate National Park near San Francisco. The park includes shoreline, redwood forests, the National Maritime Museum and the island of Alcatraz. Alcatraz served as a maximum security prison from 1933 to 1963. Native Americans reclaimed it for a time in 1968.

Where is the driest place in the U.S.?

NEVADA HAS THE LOWEST RAINFALL OF ANY STATE OF THE UNION. ONLY about 9 in (23 cm) of rain falls every year in the northeast, while around Las Vegas they get less than 4 in (10 cm). The state is dominated by the Sierra Nevada, which rises along its western border and cuts off the damp winds that blow eastwards from the Pacific Ocean.

What exploded at Frenchman's Flat and Yucca Flat?

Because Nevada has so few people, it has been used as a nuclear weapons test site. Frenchman's Flat and Yucca Flat, remote areas of southern Nevada, were used for exploding atomic bombs in 1951. In 1961 nuclear testing was banned, but in 1968 more nuclear weapons were exploded in Nevada, this time 3,800 ft (1,158 m) underground. Nuclear reactor research also began in Nevada—at the Las Vegas Bombing and Gunnery Range.

UTAH

COLORADO

NEVADA

CALIFORNIA

ARIZONA

Phoenix

Tucson

Santa Fe

Amarillo

NEW
MEXICO

Albuquerque

OKLAHOMA

Fort Worth   Dallas

Abilene

El Paso

TEXAS

Austin

Houston

San Antonio

Galveston

MEXICO

Arizona

Texas

New Mexico

What massive sign of outer space can be seen near Winslow?

Near Winslow, Arizona, is a huge crater left by a massive asteroid that collided with the Earth long ago. The crater is 4,000 ft (1,220 m) wide and 600 ft (183 m) deep. The impact would have sent up dust that blocked out the sunlight. The resulting climate change may well be the reason why the dinosaurs died out, because they depended for their food on plants that could no longer grow.

Who was William Bonney?

Billy the Kid. He was born in New York but moved to New Mexico as a child. He led a band of outlaws and claimed to have killed 27 men. Billy the Kid escaped from jail while awaiting execution and in 1881, aged 22, he was gunned down by Pat Garrett.

Where can you travel on the Devil's Road to see living organ pipes and Gila monsters?

One of Arizona's many strange habitats is the Organ Pipe Cactus National Monument, a park on the Mexican border. Here the rare organ pipe cactus grows to a height of 20 ft (6 m). The poisonous Gila monster, a type of lizard, also thrives here. A route across the Arizona desert was created around 1700 by Father Eusebio Kino, who named it El Camino del Diablo, the Devil's Road. It was a punishing route and many of the pioneers who used it died on the crossing.

What sent up a mushroom cloud at White Sands?

LOS ALAMOS IN NEW MEXICO WAS ONE OF AMERICA'S FIRST NUCLEAR WEAPONS research stations and the first atomic bomb in the world was assembled there. In 1945 the world's first nuclear weapon was detonated at White Sands, New Mexico.

White Sands, New Mexico

Why do Texans remember the Alamo?

In 1836, during the war for independence from Mexico, the Alamo, a fort in San Antonio, was occupied by 180 Americans. It was besieged by thousands of Mexican troops and every American was killed. The Texan war cry from that day was: "Remember the Alamo!"

Davy Crocket was one of the Texans besieged at the Alamo.

Where are the world's largest underground labyrinths?

The Carlsbad Caverns under the Guadelupe Mountains in New Mexico are 46,755 acres (20,000 hectares) of caves with stunning stalactites and stalagmites. 21 miles (33 km) of labyrinth have so far been explored.

What is Sky City?

An ancient site of pueblo ruins and cliff dwellings in Cibola County, New Mexico. Multi-roomed houses have been built into the caves in a sheer cliff 337 ft (101 m) high. The dwellings have mud-walled rooms—and are still inhabited today by the Acoma people.

How did a computer grow out of a radio shack?

The Tandy Corporation, based in Forth Worth, Texas, grew out of an electrical chain store named Radio Shack. In 1977 Tandy developed an affordable personal computer, the Altair 800. It was the first computer to have a keyboard like the ones used today.

What plants and animals thrive in the desert?

ARIZONA, NEW MEXICO AND TEXAS HAVE RARE DESERT PLANTS. A hundred species of cacti thrive here, as does the mesquite bush, a small spiny tree of the pea family. The agave and its close relation the yucca are tall plants that preserve water in their fleshy, waxy leaves. The creosote bush, as its name implies, has leaves that give off a strong smell of creosote. Animal life is varied too—there are coyotes, mountain lions, wildcats, and various deer as well as scorpions, rattlesnakes, and lots of birds.

How many flags have flown over Texas?

Six! From 1519 to 1685 it was Spanish. In 1685 France claimed it for a short time, then in 1691 Spain retrieved it. Mexico was the next state to claim sovereignty, then from 1836 to 1845 it was independent. In 1845 it joined the union—but from 1861 to 1865 it was part of the confederacy!

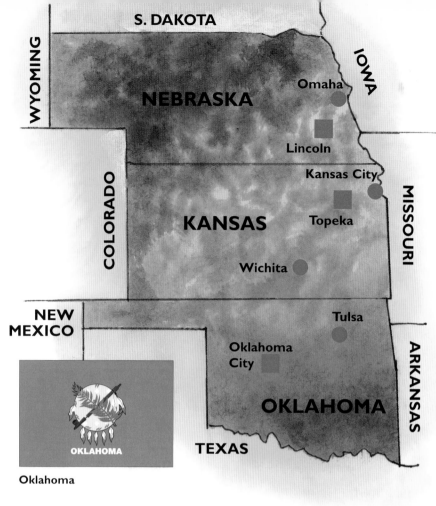

Nebraska

Kansas

Oklahoma

Why would you recognize Scott's Bluff and Chimney Rock?

Because they are famous landmarks on the old Oregon Trail, and have appeared in hundreds of westerns. Chimney Rock is a sandstone pinnacle near the Platte River in Nebraska. Pioneer groups often camped beside it. Scott's Bluff in the west of Nebraska is a cliff 800 ft (244 m) tall. The Pony Express passed by it.

Where are the Glass Mountains?

Near Fairview in Oklahoma, the mountains are covered in tiny selenite crystals, which from a distance makes them sparkle like glass. This is why they are known as the Glass Mountains, or sometimes the Gloss Mountains.

What is Arbor Day?

When the pioneers arrived in Nebraska they discovered that there were very few trees. Arbor Day (the name comes from the Latin for tree) was invented by J. Sterling Morton, a journalist who later became Secretary for Agriculture. On the very first Arbor Day in 1872 over a million trees were planted—Nebraska's present-day forests owe their existence largely to this day.

Why is Oklahoma the Sooner State?

For 50 years Oklahoma was banned to white settlers. It was set aside as an area for the Native Americans who had chosen not to fight the white people who took their land. At that time Oklahoma was called Indian Territory. But in 1889 the government decided to break their agreement and open up the land for white settlers. Lots of settlers could not wait for the official date, so to get their hands on the best land they moved in sooner than was allowed. Hence the name.

Where can you see dinosaur footprints?

In the west of Oklahoma is an area known as the panhandle, a little strip of land that sticks out along the northern border of Texas. This area has the biggest range of dinosaur fossils in America. In creek beds here you can see dinosaur footprints made 200 million years ago.

How did Turkey Red transform the Great Plains?

THE GREAT PLAINS ARE THE RICH FARMING LANDS OF OKLAHOMA, Kansas, and Nebraska. But their very dry summers often meant that farmers lost all their crops to drought. When Mennonite settlers from Russia arrived in the Great Plains, they brought with them a special hardy type of wheat named Turkey Red. The Russian wheat was tough enough to survive the winter in the Great Plains—it could be planted in autumn and was ready to harvest before the drought set in. By the early 1900s Turkey Red was the main crop in the Great Plains.

Who were the Okies?

These were the Oklahoman farmers who were driven off their land by the great dust bowl—a combination of drought and winds that reduced the land to whirling dust where nothing would grow. The poverty-stricken families trekked across America to find work—but the economic depression made their task very difficult.

What started the American Civil War?

The American Civil War was caused mainly by a quarrel over slavery. The war lasted from 1861 to 1865 and was fought between the northern and the southern states of the U.S.. The economy of the southern states relied on black slaves shipped from Africa to work in the cotton plantations and on the farms of wealthy white owners. The northern states knew that slavery was wrong, and wanted it banned. A law named the Kansas Nebraska Act, passed in 1854, said that these two southern states could decide if they wanted slavery or not. This caused an almighty row to blow up, which eventually resulted in civil war.

Why were the five civilized tribes cruelly treated?

The Cherokees, Creeks, Choctaws, Chickasaws, and Seminoles were named "civilized" by European settlers because they agreed to the white man taking their lands, adopted white customs, and learned to read and write. In exchange for giving up their rich homelands to the whites, they were given a barren area—Oklahoma. They settled there and managed to survive. But when the whites saw the land could be lived on after all, they changed their minds. In 1889 they claimed most of Oklahoma too, pushing the "civilized" tribes into even smaller tracts of land.

Many people were forced to pack up their homes and move on to find work.

Who shed blood at Gettysberg?

IN 1863 GETTYSBURG WAS THE SCENE OF THE BLOODIEST BATTLE OF THE American Civil War. Confederacy troops from the southern states invaded Union territory and threatened the crossroads town of Gettysburg in Pennsylvania. 28,000 Confederate men and 23,000 Union soldiers from the northern states were killed or wounded. The battle took three days, and though the Confederates came close to winning, in the end they lost both the battle and the war.

Which state has more professional sports teams than any other in America?

Pennsylvania, with seven professional sports teams. They are the Philadelphia Phillies and Pittsburgh Pirates in baseball, the 76ers in basketball, the Pittsburgh Steelers and Philadelphia Eagles in football, and an ice hockey team—the Pittsburgh Penguins.

What was the first capital of the United States?

New York. During the War of Independence New York was one of the leading states. It was the 11th state to ratify the constitution. George Washington's inauguration ceremony took place in New York.

How much did Peter Minuit pay for Manhattan?

When Peter Minuit arrived in America in 1626 Manhattan Island was occupied by the Wappinger Native Americans. He traded the island for some trinkets—worth about $24. The Wappinger thought they were selling the right to share the island—but the tricksy Dutch settler insisted it was a purchase.

Where were America's first department stores?

Pennsylvania. John Wanamaker opened America's first department store in the 1870s in Philadelphia. Later, Frank Woolworth opened his five-and-ten-cent stores in Lancaster. Other chain stores were also founded in Pennsylvania—Kress, Kresge, Newberry's, and Grants.

Who was America's first woman doctor?

When Elizabeth Blackwell decided to become a doctor, she could not get a school to accept her because she was a woman, and so she studied privately. Eventually the Geneva Medical School in western New York recognized her abilities and enrolled her. She graduated top of her class in 1849.

Manhattan is a center of broadcasting, publishing, and entertainment.

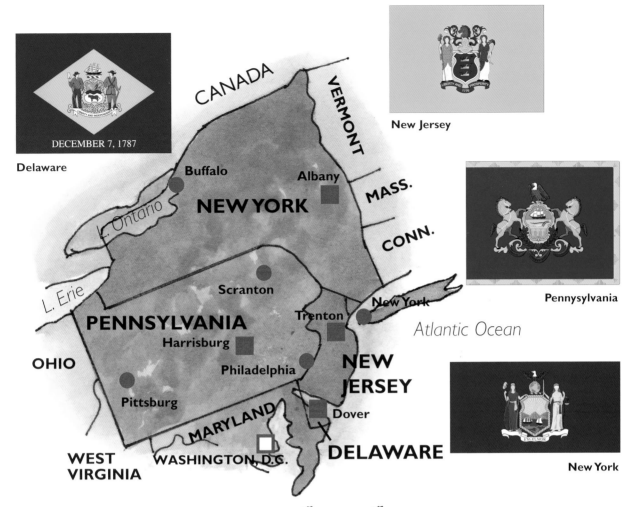

DECEMBER 7, 1787

Delaware

New Jersey

Pennysylvania

New York

CANADA

VERMONT

Buffalo

Albany

NEW YORK

MASS.

L. Ontario

CONN.

L. Erie

Scranton

New York

Trenton

Atlantic Ocean

PENNSYLVANIA

Harrisburg

NEW JERSEY

OHIO

Philadelphia

Pittsburg

Dover

MARYLAND

WEST VIRGINIA

WASHINGTON, D.C.

DELAWARE

Where did knickerbockers first get together?

At Hoboken, New Jersey, during the first ever organized game of baseball! The game was invented in 1839 by a West Point cadet. It received its official set of rules in 1845 when the Knickerbocker Baseball Club of New York City was founded. In 1846 the New York Knickerbockers played their historic first game against the Hoboken Knickerbocker Giants.

Which state is almost completely surrounded by water?

New Jersey! Well over 90 per cent of its border is water. The Delaware River forms its western border, Delaware Bay and the Atlantic lie to the south, while its northeastern border follows the Hudson River. Only 50 miles (80 km) of the state border is land—where it joins with New York.

What have Morse Code, the light bulb, and the submarine got in common?

THEY WERE ALL INVENTED IN NEW JERSEY. IN 1838 SAMUEL B. MORSE, AN ARTIST BY training, patented the first magnetic telegraph. The line ran from Washington to Baltimore, New Jersey, and the first transmitted message read: "What hath God wrought?" Forty years later another New Jerseyman, Thomas Alva Edison, lit the first electric light bulb. In 1881 the New Jerseyman John P. Holland launched the first submarine. This and later submarines were double-hulled and carried jet-propelled torpedoes. Some of them were used in World War I.

Which state relies on lobsters and chickens?

MAINE IS REALLY FAMOUS FOR ITS DELICIOUS LOBSTERS—AND ITS broiler chickens are sold all around the United States. The chickens are reared and exported and the lobsters are pulled out of the waters of the Atlantic Ocean. Fishing has always been a big industry in Maine and the lobsters are one of the main reasons for that success.

What is a Rhode Island Red?
It's a chicken first bred in Rhode Island in 1895. The bird is very distinctive with red-brown feathers, and is equally valued for its eggs and its meat.

The Rhode Island Red was developed from Asian chickens.

Which teacher went into outer space?
She was a social studies teacher in Concord, New Hampshire, who in 1985 applied to become a member of the space shuttle team. She would have become the first teacher to go into outer space. But the shuttle *Challenger* exploded over the Atlantic Ocean a few seconds after take-off, killing everyone on board.

The Pilgrim Fathers landed at Cape Cod, Massachusetts, in 1620.

Which is America's oldest university?
Harvard University was founded in 1636 in Cambridge, Massachusetts. It is named after John Harvard, who donated books and money to the school. Harvard has an impressive list of ex-students, including John F. Kennedy, e.e. cummings, Robert Frost and T.S. Eliot, Janet Reno, Mary Robinson, and the actor Tommy Lee Jones.

Where is America's oldest synagogue?
It's the Touro Synagogue in Newport, Rhode Island, built between 1759 and 1763. From its earliest days Rhode Island was known for its tolerance of all religious faiths. The Touro Synagogue is now a national monument.

Vermont

Maine

New Hampshire

CANADA

MAINE

Augusta

Montpelier

VERMONT

NEW HAMPSHIRE

Portland

Atlantic
Ocean

NEW YORK

Concord

Rhode Island

MASSACHUSETTS

Boston

Providence

RHODE ISLAND

CONNECTICUT

Hartford

Massachusetts

Connecticut

Which tea party ended in tears?

THE BOSTON TEA PARTY WAS THE EVENT
THAT TRIGGERED THE WAR OF
Independence. In 1773 Britain passed an act forcing
American settlers to pay tax on tea to Britain. In protest, a
group of men calling themselves the Sons of Liberty boarded
the English ship *Dartmouth* in Boston Harbor. There they held
a "tea party" by throwing its cargo of 342 chests of tea
overboard. The British government responded with
punishments against the state and very shortly afterwards
war broke out between the British and the settlers.

Where was the first English settlement in America?

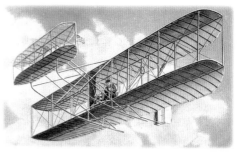

The Wrights' airplane was built in a bicycle factory.

THE VIRGINIA COMPANY OF LONDON SENT OUT THREE SHIPS TO ESTABLISH a colony in America and find something profitable to send back to England. In 1607 the sailors established Jamestown on Chesapeake Bay, Virginia. After three years of hardship they were ready to return home, but the colony was saved when its new governor, Lord De La Warr, arrived from England with supplies. In 1612 the settlers began tobacco farming, and from that time the colony thrived.

Who took to the air at Kill Devil Hills?

The first powered manned flight in the world took place in 1903 at Kill Devil Hills in North Carolina. The aircraft was built by the Wright brothers and had a gasoline engine, a propeller, and two parallel sets of wings. Orville Wright flew the plane while his brother Wilbur lay alongside the engine on the lower wing. The plane flew 120 ft (36 m).

Which state heard the first gunshots of the Civil War?

On December 20, 1860, South Carolina seceded from the Union. It was the first state to drop out. Ten others followed. The first shots of the Civil War were fired in South Carolina by Confederate troops.

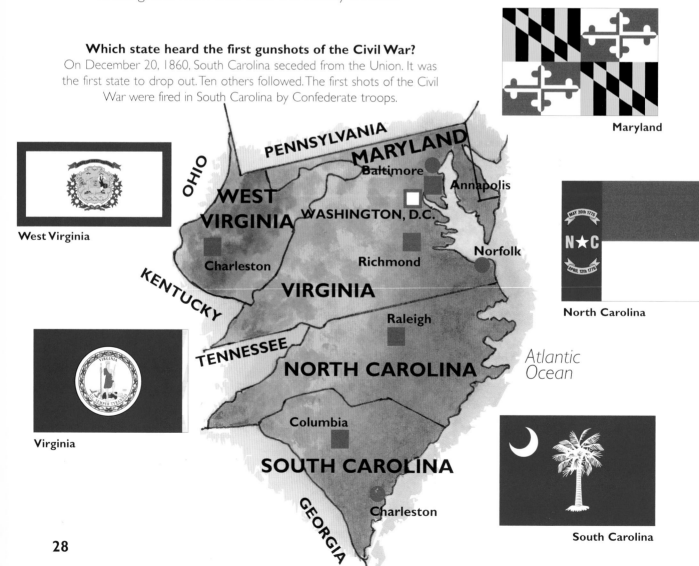

Maryland

West Virginia

North Carolina

Virginia

South Carolina

OHIO
PENNSYLVANIA
MARYLAND
Baltimore
Annapolis
WEST VIRGINIA
WASHINGTON, D.C.
Charleston
Richmond
Norfolk
KENTUCKY
VIRGINIA
Raleigh
TENNESSEE
NORTH CAROLINA
Atlantic Ocean
Columbia
SOUTH CAROLINA
GEORGIA
Charleston

Baltimore is the largest city in Maryland. It is an important shipbuilding center.

What was the Trail of Tears?

The Cherokee were civilized Native Americans living peacefully in South Carolina with farms and schools and their own written language. But the whites could not tolerate living with them. The whites forced the Cherokee out of their homes and drove them west. Many of them died on route, on the Trail of Tears.

Where can a wild turkey find refuge?

Wild turkeys used to flourish in South Carolina, but over the years they were hunted almost to extinction. Now there is a turkey refuge in South Carolina in the Francis Marion National Forest. Here turkeys are bred and released into the wild. As a result of this breeding program, the state-wide population of wild turkeys has grown dramatically.

How did John Brown die for human rights?

JOHN BROWN WAS A LEADER IN THE FIGHT AGAINST SLAVERY. IN 1859 HE AND A party of 21 men attacked a federal arsenal (weapons store) at Harper's Ferry, West Virginia. He wanted the weapons to liberate slaves. Brown and his courageous men took hostage the 60 soldiers stationed in the arsenal. The U.S. Marines were sent against them and Brown's men surrendered, but only after two of his sons had been killed. Brown was tried and hanged for inciting rebellion, and for treason and murder.

What was the Dred Scott Case?

Dred Scott, a slave, lived for a time in the slave state of Missouri and then in the free state of Wisconsin. In 1857 Scott claimed he was free man. The Supreme Court decided against him. It also decided that slavery was legal everywhere in the U.S. This case was one of the causes of the Civil War.

Which megastar had his home at Memphis?

BORN IN TUPELO, MISSISSIPPI, ELVIS PRESLEY MOVED TO MEMPHIS, TENNESSEE, AS A teenager. When he became a superstar he bought Graceland, a mansion just outside the town. He lived there with his wife, and then during the years that he spent alone. It was at Graceland that he died of heart failure in 1977. The mansion is now a site of pilgrimage for his millions of fans. Elvis was the highest-paid performer in the history of show business.

When can a horse win a crown in Kentucky?

The most important and popular event of the year in Kentucky is the Kentucky Derby, which is part of the Triple Crown in the horse-racing calendar. The first Derby was run in 1867 at Churchill Downs in Louisville, Kentucky.

Where can you visit a diamond mine?

The only state in the U.S. to have produced diamonds is Arkansas, which has a diamond on its flag. Diamonds were first discovered there in 1906. Today the Crater of Diamonds State Park is open to the public. It is the only diamond mine in the world to admit visitors.

Why are Fulbright students always on the move?

The Fulbright scholarship is an exchange program that helps American students to study abroad and students from overseas to study in America. It is open to graduates, and was started by Senator J. William Fulbright of Arkansas in 1946. From 1966 teachers and researchers could also apply for study grants.

What was the "monkey trial"?

In the early years of this century a biologist named Charles Darwin claimed that people were descended from apes. This upset the Church, which taught that Adam and Eve were our first ancestors. The Church was very strong in the state of Tennessee, and a law was passed there making it illegal to teach Darwin's theories in schools. But in the early 1920s John Scopes, a biology teacher in Dayton, Tennessee, began to tell his students that people were descended from apes. In 1925 he was charged with breaking the law and fined $100 in a famous trial that became known as the "monkey trial."

Elvis Presley is probably the most famous entertainer of the 20th century.

Who named Kentucky paradise?

Daniel Boone was a famous pioneer and hunter in the early days of American settlement. He loved the Kentucky countryside, where he saw herds of buffalo roaming across the plains, vast tracts of forest alive with deer and wild turkeys, and rivers full of fish. To him Kentucky was a hunter's paradise.

Where was the most violent earthquake ever recorded in the U.S.?

At New Madrid, Missouri, in the winter of 1811 to 1812. The quake registered from Canada to the Gulf of Mexico and there were 1,874 aftershocks. Although the quake measured 8.4 on the Richter scale, fortunately very few people were killed.

Kentucky

Why is Kentucky named the Bluegrass State?

Although Kentucky's major crops are hemp and tobacco it is known as the Bluegrass State after the great high stands of bluish-colored grasses that grow around the Lexington/Lafayette area.

Missouri

IOWA

ILLINOIS

INDIANA

OHIO

WEST VIRGINIA

VIRGINIA

NORTH CAROLINA

Louisville

Frankfort

St Louis

Jefferson City

KANSAS

MISSOURI

KENTUCKY

Knoxville

Nashville

TENNESSEE

ARKANSAS

Memphis

OKLAHOMA

Little Rock

MISSISSIPPI

ALABAMA

GEORGIA

TEXAS

LOUISIANA

Tennessee

Arkansas

The Gateway Arch in St. Louis is a memorial to the pioneers of the West.

What happened to Captain Cook in Hawaii?

In 1778 Captain Cook arrived in Hawaii and named the islands the Sandwich Islands after his sponsor, the Earl of Sandwich. He got on well with the islanders until 1779, when they quarreled over the theft of one of the Captain's boats. Going ashore to recover his boat from the thief, Cook was ambushed in a fight and killed.

HAWAII

Honolulu

Hawaii

Pacific Ocean

What was the worst natural disaster in U.S. history?

In 1992, Hurricane Andrew hit the coast of Florida and devastated Florida City and a town named Homestead. It then went on to the Gulf Coast states, where Morgan City and Lafayette in Louisiana suffered terrible damage. In all, Hurricane Andrew caused $20 billion worth of damage and left an estimated 40 dead.

Where did people live in a cave for 8,000 years?

The Russell Caves near Bridgeport, Alabama, extend miles into the mountainside. The cave closest to the entrance shows signs that humans must have lived there for over 8,000 years. The caves were declared a national monument in 1961.

Which town does Oprah Winfrey call home?

OPRAH WINFREY WAS BORN IN KOSCIUSKO, MISSISSIPPI, IN 1954, and began her TV career as a co-anchor on the evening news at Nashville TV. By 1978 she had moved on to talk shows and soon hosted her own Oprah Winfrey Show. She will talk about absolutely anything, which has made her enormously popular. She has her own production company and has starred in two movies, *The Color Purple*, for which she was nominated for an Oscar, and *Beloved*. The Oprah Winfrey Show is seen all over the world.

Why do people flock to Florida?

Over 5,000 people move to Florida each year. It has more newcomers than any other state and the fourth biggest population in the U.S.. Many newcomers are retired people who move there to enjoy the sunshine. Many others are refugees from Cuba or Haiti seeking work.

Who erected a monument to a boll weevil?

The boll weevil is a bug that eats the heart of the cotton seed, destroying the crop. Many southern states grew nothing but cotton until 1915, when a plague of boll weevils ate everything and forced them to grow different things. Although 1915 was a disaster for the farmers, when they grew more crops in following years, they were better off. So in gratitude, the farmers of Enterprise, Alabama, erected a monument to the boll weevil.

The Mississippi River was used as a major transport route by Union forces in the Civil War.

Alabama

Georgia

Where do trees have their roots in the air?

T HE EVERGLADES NATIONAL PARK IN FLORIDA IS A VAST SALTWATER swamp full of mangrove trees. It gets its magical name because it seems like an endless expanse of green glades. Mangrove trees thrive in tidal salt water. When the tide goes out, their roots are exposed to the air. Alligators bask in the swamp and the trees are home to spoonbills, brown pelicans, ospreys, and bald eagles.

TENNESSEE

ARKANSAS

LOUISIANA

MISSISSIPPI

Atlanta

Birmingham

ALABAMA

Jackson

GEORGIA

Savannah

Montgomery

Mobile

Tallahassee

Jacksonville

Atlantic Ocean

New Orleans

Baton Rouge

Gulf of Mexico

FLORIDA

Tampa

Miami

Florida

Cape Canaveral, Florida

Louisiana

Mississippi

Who wrote about a mockingbird?

Harper Lee was born in Monroeville, Alabama. Although she studied law, she became an airline ticket clerk before quitting her job to become a writer. Her novel *To Kill A Mockingbird* won the Pulitzer Prize in 1961 and was made into a movie starring Gregory Peck. It is about the trial of an innocent black man.

Who were the first Americans to shoot briefly into space?

Cape Canaveral in Florida is America's major launch site for most of its space exploration projects. In 1961 Alan Shepard took off from here on the first manned American flight. It was suborbital and lasted 15 minutes. The following year, John Glenn became the first American to orbit the earth. His flight lasted just 4 minutes 55 seconds.

Which Dayton brothers pioneered air travel?

THE WRIGHT BROTHERS MADE THEIR FIRST POWERED FLIGHT IN NORTH CAROLINA, but they lived and designed their planes in Dayton, Ohio. The brothers lived together all their lives and enjoyed mechanics from a very young age. They opened a bicycle repair shop and also made their own bicycles. It was a short leap from bicycles to gliders. They built their first glider in 1900 and went on to construct the first manned powered airplane.

What was the worst air disaster in the U.S.?
In 1979 an engine fell off a DC 10 as it was taking off from O' Hare Airport, Chicago. The plane flew out of control and crashed. All 273 people on board were killed.

Chicago is famous for its architecture. The world's first skyscraper was built there in 1885.

How did Toni win world recognition?
Toni Morrison grew up in Lorain, Ohio and attended Harvard and Cornell Universities. Her novel *Beloved* won the 1987 Pulitzer Prize and in 1993 she won the Nobel Prize for Literature.

Why was Anthony Wayne mad?
Mad Anthony Wayne was an early pioneer who got his nickname when he stormed a British fort in a surprise night attack. He fought against the Native Americans in the Battle of Fallen Timbers, and helped drive them out of their homelands in Ohio, Indiana, Michigan, and Illinois.

Why did Ohio and Michigan nearly go to war?
Ohio and Michigan both claimed they owned an area around Toledo. In 1836 the two states called out their armies and were ready to fight. Then Congress gave the area to Ohio—and it gave Michigan some land in the Upper Peninsula. So both states were happy again.

What made Sarah Breedlove rich?
Born in 1867 in Louisiana, Sarah Breedlove invented a formula for straightening curly hair. She began by selling her product from door to door in 1905. Her business grew and she opened the Madam C. Walker Manufacturing Company in Indianapolis. Sarah Breedlove was the first black American woman in the U.S. to become a millionaire.

Where is America's largest prison?
Mississippi. Its State Penitentiary is the largest in America with a total of 1,536 inmates. Ohio has the second largest Federal Correctional Institute in the U.S. with a population of 47,248, then comes Michigan Federal Correctional Institution with 43,784 residents, and then Illinois with 40,425.

Michigan

Ohio

Illinois

Indiana

Who is Steveland Judkins Morris?

He is better known as Stevie Wonder. He was born blind in Saginaw, Michigan, in 1950. By age 13 he had his own recording contract and was known as "Little Stevie Wonder." During the 1970s and 1980s he produced many smash hits, recording them in Detroit on the Tamla Motown record label.

One of Stevie Wonder's biggest hits was *Superstition*.

Who was the first woman to run for presidency of the U.S.?

VICTORIA CLAFLIN WOODHULL (1838–1927) WAS BORN IN

Homer, Ohio. She was a feminist and social reformer, and the first woman to be nominated as a presidential candidate. She stood for the presidency in 1872 as a representative of the Equal Rights Party. She was not elected. She believed in equal rights, but she also supported the idea of eugenics—which means allowing only beautiful and intelligent people to have children.

Native Americans

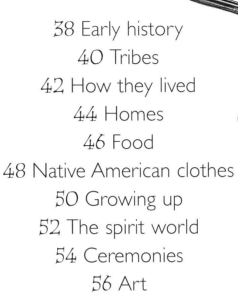

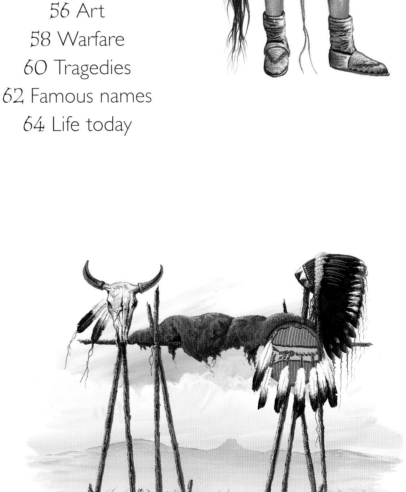

Who left behind only their burial mounds?

The Hopewell people lived in the valleys of Ohio and Illinois for 1,500 years from 800 B.C. The little that is known about their culture comes from objects found in their burial mounds. These mounds reached over 30 ft (10 m) in height, and as much as 200 ft (70 m) around.

Who first discovered America?

Pottery, stone ornaments, and clay images have been found in Hopewell burial mounds.

MANY THOUSANDS OF YEARS BEFORE CHRISTOPHER COLUMBUS SAILED

across the Atlantic from Europe, people trekked into North America across a land bridge from Siberia. This happened some 10 to 12,000 years ago, when the Ice Age was coming to an end. Some historians also believe that people might have been living in South America over 30,000 years ago. Some of these people may have moved north into the southwestern United States.

Why were Native Americans called "Indians"?

Before America was known to Europeans, the explorer Christopher Columbus planned to travel around the world and reach India by sailing west. After a journey lasting over two months, he finally reached land—probably the Bahamas—and thinking he had reached India, called the people there Indians! The name stuck and became a label for all the different Native Americans living in the New World.

Columbus meets non Europeans in the New World.

Who had a good government before the Europeans?

Five tribes, former enemies, came together and formed the Iroquois Confederacy in the early 1600s. Decisions were made by a council who were all men and elected for life, but women had the right to fire any councillor.

Cornplanter, an Iroquois chief.

How many Native Americans lived in America before Europeans arrived?

Impossible to know for sure. Some historians estimate under 1.5 million Native Americans. But others say these numbers are ridiculously low for such a vast land mass. They give figures of between 8 and 18 million.

Whose name means "those who have vanished?"

The Hohokam people, who lived in the Arizona desert, near the border with Mexico, over 2,000 years ago. They survived by building canals and farming. They were given their name by the Pima people who later came into the region where "those who have vanished" once lived.

Who were the Mogollon and the Mimbres?

The Hohokam are not the only Native Americans who have vanished from the southwestern United States. The Mogollon people lived in the mountains on the Arizona—New Mexico border. The Mimbres also lived in this region, but by around 1300, like the Mogollon, they were extinct.

What started at 4 a.m. in 1607?

The first permanent English settlement in the United States. One settler said "About foure in the morning, wee descried the Land of Virginia." And the settler went on to exclaim how they: "...got good store of Mussels and Oysters, which lay upon the ground as thicke as stones."

Who was inspired by the Iroquois government?

Benjamin Franklin, co-author of the Constitution. He thought the idea of a government like the Iroquois Confederacy could be used by the English colonies. The eagle on the United States shield is the Iroquois bald eagle—also a symbol for the Iroquois nation.

Where did Native Americans get their horses?

FOR A LONG TIME, IT WAS THOUGHT THERE WERE NO HORSES IN NORTH AMERICA until the Spanish brought them in the 1550s. But fossil records show evidence of horses long before Europeans arrived. At some unknown date they disappeared, only to be reintroduced by the Spanish.

Was there really a Sioux tribe?

No. The word Sioux was adopted by French explorers who picked it up from the Chippewa tribe. Sioux is a Chippewa word for "enemy." The Chippewa used it to describe the Lakota people, whom they had pushed westward from the Western Great Lakes, where the Lakota originally lived. So the Sioux are really the Lakota, a name that means "where the people of peace dwell."

Who were the five civilized tribes?

THE CHOCTAW, CHEROKEE, CREEK, CHICKSAW, AND SEMINOLE TRIBES,

living in the Southeast of North America, were called the "Five Civilized Tribes" by early white settlers. They were given this name because of similarities between their cultures and those of the Europeans. The tribes lived in planned villages, were farmers as well as hunters, and some were wealthy enough to own slaves. Later, some of them became Christians and adopted other aspects of the settlers' lives.

Which tribes hunted buffalo?

The Blackfeet, Cheyenne, Comanche, Crow, and Lakota people all lived on the Great Plains, a large area stretching from the Mississippi River to the Rocky Mountains and from Canada to Texas. Although they had important differences, they lived by hunting herds of buffalo on the prairies.

Osceola was the leader of the Seminole people of what is now Florida and Georgia.

Which tribe worked together as one large family?

The Creek divided their land into family plots, but the work of farming was carried out by all of them working together as equals, including their chief. Some of the harvest was stored in a special building and shared for public occasions.

What is special about the Seminole of Florida?

They are a mixed group, formed from the survivors of various Florida tribes after the European slave trade had almost wiped them out. Mostly Creek, they were joined by runaway black slaves and successfully resisted attempts to root them out from the swampland.

What tribe believe the number seven to be sacred?

The Cherokee hold seven ritual ceremonies, six of which took place annually and the seventh every seven years. They had seven "mother towns," originally the headquarters of their seven clans.

Which tribe hunted and farmed by the Missouri River in North Dakota?

The Mandans hunted the buffalo like other Plains people, but they also lived in permanent villages built high up on the banks of the Missouri. They farmed the land and grew maize. The explorers Lewis and Clark spent a winter living with the Mandans before heading west.

Where did the Apache come from?

THEY CAME FROM NORTHWESTERN CANADA WHERE THEY HAD LIVED as hunters and where farming was impossible. Their migration to the Southwest began around A.D.1000 and continued over the next 500 years.

Which western state is named after a tribe?

Utah is named after the Utes, a people who lived on the edge of the Plains and the Great Basin. Oklahoma comes from "okla homma," which means "home of the red people."

Which tribe helped two Americans explore west of the Mississippi?

President Thomas Jefferson invited Lewis and Clark to explore this unknown land. With the help of the Nez Perce people, who built canoes for them and drew maps of the rivers, they succeeded in reaching the Pacific.

Who had tails on their boats?

The Mandan people built the frame of a one-person boat out of willow branches and covered it with buffalo hide. They left the buffalo's tail on the hide and attached a piece of wood to it, so the boat had a built-in rudder.

Who hunted with duck decoys?

In northwestern Nevada hunters made decoy ducks out of grasses and plant stalks. They floated them on lakes and marshes within bow-shooting distance of the hunter's hide. Migrating birds, deceived into thinking it was safe to land, became sitting ducks for the hunters' arrows!

Who could not live without the birch?

Tribes who lived in the northeast of North America used the wood of birch trees for building their wigwams and canoes. The bark of the birch was tough and weatherproof, so they used it for making baskets and storage vessels.

Many Native American tribes could not have survived without horses.

What sport had up to 200 players?

PEOPLE OF THE SOUTHEAST, ESPECIALLY THE CHOCTAW, WERE FANATICAL players of a stick-and-ball game played with large teams. French settlers thought the stick looked like a bishop's crosier. So when they introduced it to Europe, they called it La Crosse, hence the game known today as lacrosse.

Who liked giving things away?

Better-off families of Pacific coast tribes demonstrated their wealth by holding potlatch ceremonies and handing out gifts to their guests, which could number over 100. The worth of a gift depended on the status of the guest. The hosts expected to get back the worth of their gifts by being invited to potlatches held by their guests. Although potlatches became illegal in the 1900s, they still take place today.

Who hunted for heavyweight prey?

The Plains people lived by hunting the mighty buffalo. It was about 6 ft (2 m) high, and despite its tremendous weight 1 ton (1,000 kg), could still run very fast in a stampede. Before horses were used, Plains hunters tried to sneak up on buffalo downwind, disguised in animal skins. Another extremely dangerous technique was to stampede the buffalo over cliffs or into pens. On horseback, the buffalo was brought down with spears, and bows and arrows tipped with iron or stone. Bows were specially strengthened and shortened to under 3 ft (1 m) for easier use on horseback.

How did Native Americans record history?

They painted a record of past events in picture-writing and symbols on animal hides. They also passed stories on by word-of-mouth. Many people memorized the tribe's history to pass it on to the next generation.

How valuable were eagle feathers?

Around 1850, a valuable horse could be exchanged for 15 eagle feathers. Their value came from their scarcity and religious importance. Especially valuable were the more colorful feathers of young eagles that took a long time to capture. Prized feathers decorated headdresses and costumes.

Did the tribes trade with one another?

Yes, at fixed times of the year tribes came together at special meeting places to trade. Nomadic people from the Plains with surplus buffalo skins would trade them for farm produce from settled tribes.

Who did not bury the dead?

SOME OF THE PLAINS TRIBES CONSTRUCTED scaffolding, or used trees, to hold the body above ground, safe from wild animals while it decayed. The Huron people placed the body in a coffin and kept it above the ground on poles for up to 12 years before the bones were buried.

Possessions, like this warrior's headdress and feathers, were left close to the corpse.

The apartments of the Pueblo tribes.

Who lived in longhouses?

Iroquois tribes lived in groups of up to 100 people in long and narrow houses. These houses were about 25 ft (7.5 m) wide and 150 ft (45 m) long, built using wooden poles covered with strips of tree bark. Platforms added to the walls indoors were used as beds and benches, and the earthen floors were covered with more bark or woven mats. Partitions divided one family area from another, but "neighbors" sometimes shared a cooking fire.

Who welcomed the morning Sun from the rooftops?

The Mandans lived in domed timber lodges with layers of grass and sods of earth on the rafters. Such a sturdy structure could easily support the weight of the village elders, who had a tradition of climbing on the rooftops at dawn to greet each day.

Did the Native Americans have toothbrushes and hairbrushes?

Of course! Porcupine hairs were used for bristles and sometimes a stick was cut into the right shape and frayed at the edges to make a toothbrush. The tail of a porcupine was cut and crafted to make a hairbrush.

Who were the first Americans to live in "apartments"?

SOME 700 YEARS AGO, THE ANASAZI PEOPLE STARTED BUILDING apartmentlike blocks out of adobe (unburned, sun-dried bricks). The apartments rose up in canyons and at the entrances to caves in Arizona and New Mexico. Ruins of one large site, Pueblo Bonito, show that well over 1,000 people lived here. In the 1500s, Pueblo tribes also built rows of adobe houses up to five stories high. They reached the upper stories by climbing connecting ladders. Native Americans still live in some of these adobe houses.

Who lived in thatched houses?

The Choctaw people, who lived in the semitropical climate of the Southeast. They used the leaves of the palmetto, a small palm tree, as a thatch for their houses. This allowed the air to circulate better than any wood, stone, or brick, and prevented the house from becoming uncomfortably hot inside.

What are sweat lodges?

Plains tribes used these for religious ceremonies. They were windowless and dome-shaped. Inside the lodge, a collection of large stones was set over a fire to generate heat and steam.

Two Blackfeet women with a child on a horse-drawn frame called a travois.

What is a hogan?

THE NAVAJO PEOPLE OF THE SOUTHWEST LIVED IN BEEHIVE-SHAPED HOUSES

called hogans. The frame of a hogan was built with poles of pinewood, or sometimes stone. Then the hogan was covered with a layer of dried mud. The Navajo still like to have a hogan on their land, close to their more modern house. Many still live just in hogans.

How was dried buffalo dung used inside a tepee?

It made a useful fuel for cooking and for keeping warm, because when it burned it was almost smokeless. The little smoke produced by the fire escaped through a gap at the top of the tepee created by cutting open a flap in the buffalo hide.

The inside of a tepee was warm and comfortable.

Spearing fish required patience
and skill.

Who has boomerangs that do not come back?
The Hopi people use a curved stick, about the same size as a boomerang, to throw through the air and bring down rabbits. Hopi hunters gather in a large circle, up to a mile wide, and move forward together. When a rabbit appears, a nearby hunter throws his stick.

How was food boiled without saucepans?
Simple. A hole was dug, lined with rawhide to prevent leaking, and filled with water into which red-hot stones were dropped. The stones made the water hot enough to boil meat, with more stones from the fire being added as necessary.

What did the Navajo learn from the Spanish?
The Navajo used to be nomadic hunters, but they learned about farming crops and sheep from the Spanish, who arrived in the 1500s. At first, the Navajo stole sheep from the Spanish, then in time they became expert sheep farmers.

What can you find to eat in a desert?
More than you might think. The fruit of most cacti is edible. Some cactus fruit needs cooking, but the prickly pears can be eaten fresh once their thorns have been removed. Some cactus seeds can be pounded to make flour, and a number of edible roots can be dug out from underground.

What are the three sisters?

MAIZE, BEANS, AND SQUASH WERE
CALLED THE THREE SISTERS BY
the Iroquois. They were so important as sources of food
that they were thought of as female spirits. Maize (corn)
was a valuable source of carbohydrate, beans were a source
of protein, and squash provided important vitamins.
European settlers learned to grow pumpkins from
Native Americans, and made it into one of their
traditional foods for Thanksgiving—sweet pumpkin pie.

How do you keep antelope meat?

The meat of deer, antelope, turkey, and rabbit could be dried in the sun. Salt was then added as a preservative. Salt was collected from salt springs by boiling away the water, or by scraping it from a salt bed.

What was pemmican?

Pemmican was buffalo meat pounded and mixed with berries and fat to produce a type of dried food. It was stored and used later when fresh food was hard to find. Pemmican was high in protein and could be stored for years if necessary.

Who ate fast food?

The people of the Great Basin, like the Shoshone and the Paiute, lived in a land so arid it could not be farmed. They never stayed in the same place for very long, and as they moved around they lived off food that they dug from the ground. They ate grasshoppers and other insects, lizards, roots, seeds, and nuts. They were very close to their environment, but Europeans did not understand this and called them "Digger Indians."

Who hunted in disguise?

TRIBES LIKE THE CHEROKEE, CREEK, AND CHOCTAW, WHO DID NOT HAVE buffalo on their land, hunted deer instead. A solitary deer was tracked by a lone hunter, sometimes wearing a deer's hide as camouflage, and imitating a deer's mating call to attract his prey.

A Cherokee hunter approaches his prey— downwind of them.

Mohawk warriors were fearless and brave.

Who had wild hairstyles?
The Mohawks, one of the tribes that made up the Iroquois nation, had a distinctive hairstyle that remains popular with some people today. Another hairstyle was to keep one side of the scalp cleanly shaved while the other side was painted a bright color.

Why was the buffalo important to fashion?
Nearly everything the Native Americans wore was made of leather. Buffalo skin was first softened (tanned) by soaking it in water and rubbing it with fatty oils and the brains of the animal. Then it was stretched into shape across a wooden frame and dried. After scraping the hide with sandstone, the soft and supple leather could be cut and sewn into clothes. Buffalo killed later in the year had thicker hides that were more useful for making warm winter clothes.

Did Native American women wear perfume?

PERFUME WAS NOT USED, BUT WOMEN ON THE Plains liked to give a fresh scent to clean clothes by rubbing them with a herb called sweetgrass. Makeup was not common. Sometimes women painted the part in their hair red, but this was to show their age rather than to make them look beautiful.

Where do moccasins come from?

Moccasins came in many different styles—Apaches even wore long ones up to the knee.

Moccasin is an Algonquian word for the footwear made from buffalo or deer hides. The soles were made from hard, untanned skin (rawhide) while the uppers were made of soft, tanned skin. The two parts were sewed together with thread made from the sinews of the animal, and decorated with beads or colored feather quills. Moccasins were always made by women, and different tribes had their own designs.

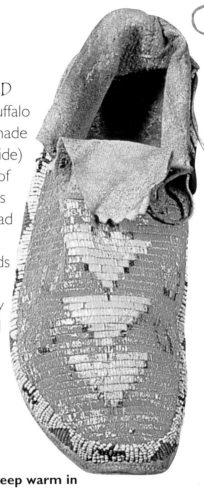

How did the Pima and Papago keep warm in the winter?

The Pima and Papago came from the deep Southwest and needed very few clothes in the hot climate. But when the temperature dropped in the winter, they kept themselves warm by rubbing animal grease on their bare upper bodies.

Were feathers worn just for fun?

Some tribes used feathers for decorative or ritual purposes. But the elaborate eagle-feather headdress of the Lakota (Sioux), which reached from head to toe, could be worn only by a warrior who had proved his courage in battle. Eagle feathers were highly prized, because they were thought to be full of spiritual power.

Where was a roach worn?

On the head—because a roach is a headdress made from dyed animal hair attached to a narrow, flat piece of bone that fits onto the head. The most important kind of roach was decorated with one or more feathers to show victory or bravery in battle.

Who walked on yucca?

The Paiute lived in an extremely dry, semidesert environment where there were no buffalo to provide leather for moccasins. However, the fibre of the yucca, a desert plant, could be woven into moccasins that were light and comfortable for the climate.

Why was a bear claw necklace highly prized?

When was the last time you tried fighting a bear? The killing of a bear was an extremely dangerous activity, and it happened so rarely that the claws were very valuable. A bear claw necklace was a highly prized piece of jewelry.

Papooses were safe and sturdy, and nicer to look at than modern ones.

How did babies travel with their parents?

In a papoose (originally an Algonquian word). The papoose was made of soft animal skin and had a stiff backboard woven from twigs. It was tied onto the mother's back and the baby was held in a comfortable upright position, able to see its surroundings. Some papooses were made with sharp, projecting, wooden points, so if they fell off while the mother was riding a horse, the points would stick in the ground and protect the baby. Heavy padding formed a sun shield over the top of the papoose and this also protected the baby's head if it fell.

Who stopped eating turtles?

Many Native American tribes had rituals for their children before they were even born. People like the Nez Perce and the Northern Shoshone had ritual prayers for men who wanted to be fathers. Pregnant mothers had their own prayers, and followed a special diet, giving up meat and eating only fish and birds. A pregnant Iroquois woman stopped eating turtles in the hope that her baby would not grow up clumsy on land, like a turtle. In Navajo communities, women untied their braided hair, and freed animals like horses hoping to create a free passage and safe birth for the baby.

Who had to kill to become a man?

PEOPLE LIKE THE CHICKSAW, CREEK, AND CHOCTAW EXPECTED A YOUNG MAN to become a man by wounding or killing an enemy in battle. Only after he had done this was the man granted an adult name and a party, held to celebrate the event.

How did Navajo girls celebrate growing up?

The first laugh of a child, and reaching the age of seven, were both marked with festivities. When a girl reached puberty, there was a ceremony called the Kinalda, in which she was covered in mud. The Kinalda still takes place today.

Which tribes trace their descent through their mothers?

Lots of tribes, including the Iroquois, Cherokee, Choctaw, Creek, Apalachee, Navajo, and Apache, trace their descent through the mother's side of their families. When an Apache male married, he always went to live in the home of his wife's mother.

What were marriages like?

A marriage among Plains tribes depended on the man being able to offer some horses as a dowry to his future father-in-law. An Iroquois man would give a present to his future wife instead, and they usually had a trial marriage before they agreed to the real thing.

How did Pueblo men prove their manhood?

Pueblo tribes organized mock battles between the young men and older men in their community. A young man had to show his courage and strength without injuring anyone, in order to be accepted as an adult.

What were dumaiyas?

AMONG THE HOPI PEOPLE, A DUMAIYA WAS A KIND of trial marriage: the woman lived with her boyfriend's family for a few days. If the family were happy with the arrangement, a more formal wedding ceremony would take place.

A buffalo hunt was dangerous but the rewards were great.

How did Plains men celebrate their first kill?

When a young man killed his first buffalo, he would be given the tastiest part, the tongue, as a reward. But the man was expected to decline the offer, and instead to share it out among his friends as a mark of generosity. In fact, to show his maturity, he wouldn't eat any of the first animal he killed.

Where is the spirit world?

Everywhere. The world of Native Americans is filled every which way with spiritual forces. The spirits are seen mostly as kindly, but sometimes as capable of harm to the human world. The spirits live in nature, and nearly everything, from a glorious eagle to a humble seed of corn, is believed to have spiritual powers. Aspects of life like illness or climate are still understood by Native Americans to be ruled by the spirits.

What are thunder pipes?

Plains tribes felt that thunder and lightning were punishments sent down on them by the spirits. They needed to get on good terms with the spirits to avoid their anger, so they got together for the ritual smoking of thunder pipes. These were colorful pipes decorated with eagle feathers and small bells.

A shaman is part doctor, psychiatrist, prophet and ghost-hunter.

What is a shaman?

SHAMANS, SOMETIMES MISTAKENLY CALLED witch-doctors, are men or women who are able to talk to the spirits and persuade them to do things. They are especially valued for their ability to heal the sick by driving out harmful spirits from the body. Shamans practice herbal medicine. They often work themselves into a trance-like state, experiencing spiritual visions.

What were masks used for?

Many tribes conducted ritual ceremonies to get in touch with the spirit world. Masks played a very important role in these ceremonies. They were designed and painted in special ways to show the spirits' nature, and help create a supernatural atmosphere.

Who made spirit dolls?

Pueblo tribes like the Hopi believed that the Kachina spirits escorted their people into life from a previous underground existence. The Hopi gave Kachina dolls to their children to teach them about the different types of spirits.

Who did the spirits command to walk backward?

Special warriors among the Lakota people were directed by spirits to lead their lives backward. They would only walk forward when they meant to go backward, and use "yes" and "no" in their opposite senses. But in battle they behaved like ordinary warriors.

Why are eagles sacred?

Eagles are admired by many tribes for their magnificence. They are thought of as messengers between the spirit world and the world of humans. Native Americans created special dances to imitate the eagle's flight.

Why is the Great Turtle important to the Iroquois?

It features in the Iroquois creation story. The Great Turtle is the supreme animal. When the world was made of only water, the turtle caught a pregnant woman who fell from the sky. The turtle dove into the deep, returned with bits of earth that fell with the woman, and helped create the world.

What were False Face societies ?

THEY WERE GROUPS OF RELIGIOUS PEOPLE LIKE SHAMANS WHO WORE SACRED masks. These masks, or false faces, were thought to draw and catch forces from the spirit world. The masks looked frightening but were worn in rituals meant to restore health to the sick.

White Buffalo was a shaman of the Blackfeet tribe.

What happened to a Cry Shed?

It was set on fire and burned down. The Cry Shed was built of earth and stood for the troubles and wishes of a community. As it went up in smoke, misfortunes were blown away on the wind and hopes and expectations carried to the spirit world.

Why did the Native Americans smoke pipes?

Pipe smoking was a social activity. Pipes were smoked at friendly gatherings with neighboring communities, and to mark important events. These might be the signing of a peace treaty between warring groups, or the arrival of an important guest. Tobacco was smoked in pipes that were sometimes specially made for the occasion.

Who was the Keeper of the Smoke?

He was the chief official at ceremonies conducted by the Papago and Pima people of Arizona. Every four years, they celebrated the bounty of another successful harvest. In their semidesert environment, the raising of crops was a matter of life and death, and the ceremony was a serious occasion.

Who enjoyed trick-or-treating?

THE IROQUOIS. THEY CELEBRATED A WINTER FESTIVAL IN WHICH small groups of teenagers were led singing and dancing around the village by an older woman. They stopped outside people's homes and waited for presents to be brought out to them.

A pipe could be smoked for peace or for war.

What was the most painful ceremony?

The Sun Dance of the Plains people involved dancers having skewers implanted in their chest muscles, and being attached by rope to the sacred cottonwood tree. In return for their pain, they hoped for a plentiful supply of buffalo to feed the community. The climax to the ceremony was a ritual dance. The uprooted cottonwood tree was painted and decorated, and some dancers hung themselves from the fork of the tree by the skewers in their chests.

What was the Green Corn ceremony?

A harvest thanksgiving ceremony that took place, and still does, among Native Americans in the Southeast and Northeast. Thirty or more people dance in pairs around a large fire, chanting ritual prayers in thanks to the spirits. Then they eat a large feast.

The ghost dance was a way of remembering the past.

Who danced the Ghost Dance?

THE GHOST DANCE WAS DEVELOPED BY FOLLOWERS of a Paiute holy man. He believed that ritual dancing would restore the old way of life enjoyed by the Native Americans before the arrival of Europeans. The dance spread to Plains tribes who did not like the way Europeans were changing their traditional life style. The dance promised the return of the buffalo and communication with the spirits of the dead. Although the Ghost Dance was peaceful, army authorities saw it as a threat and outlawed its performance.

What was the Busk?

An autumn harvest festival celebrated by the Creek, Cherokee, Choctaw, and Apalachee. It lasted four days, beginning with cleaning the village and putting out all fires. On the last day, as the climax to a communal feast, a new fire was lit to mark the start of a new farming year.

Who was the White Shell Woman?

An important Apache spirit. When a girl reached the age of marriage, a special ceremony was held for her. An adult dressed up as the White Shell woman to celebrate the girl's transition to womanhood.

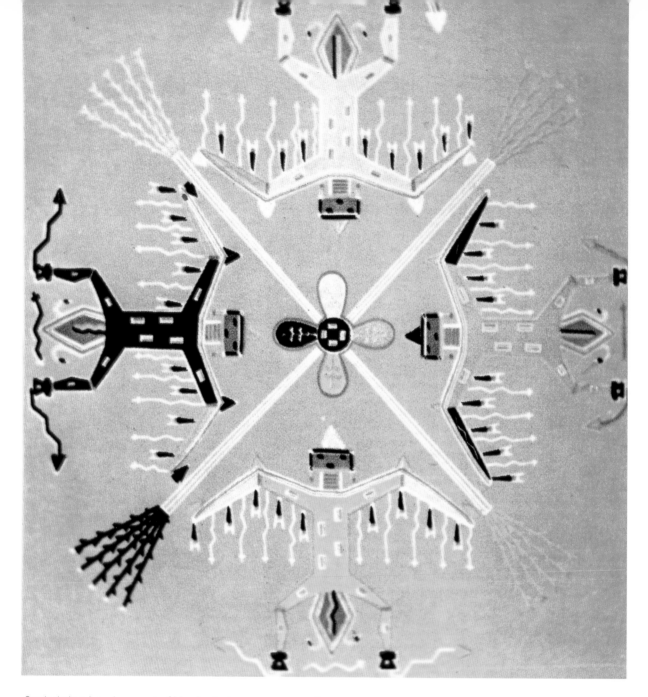

Sandpaintings have been part of Navajo ritual over many generations.

What are sand paintings?

GRAINS OF COLORED SAND ARE PAINSTAKINGLY POSITIONED TO form a complicated design of geometric shapes and symbols. Sandpaintings are a way of recording events using symbols. Today, sandpaintings are kept as works of art, but traditionally they are wiped away when the religious ritual is over.

Who made beautiful jewelry?

The Navajo became expert artistic jewelers in the 1870s. They produce fine necklaces and belts decorated with turquoise, a beautiful blue-green precious stone.

Who had beautiful battle shields?

The Crow people were famous for the care and artistry they put into their battle shields. The shields were about 2 ft (60 cm) in diameter, made of rawhide, and painted with symbols that had a personal meaning to their creator.

Who were, and still are, master potters?

Pueblo people like the Zuni and Hopi are the master potters of the Native American world. Centuries of experience have been passed down to today's generation of potters, who turn out beautifully-crafted and finely painted ceramics.

How do Native Americans make music?

Music is an essential part of religious, social, and military life. Logs were hollowed out to form drums of all sizes and the tops covered with tightly stretched animal skin. Turtle shells were turned into rattles, and hollowed bones made pipes that were blown in battle.

Who was kidnapped for blankets?

The Navajo began weaving blankets for their own use, but their work was so artistic that settlers in New Mexico kidnapped them and forced them to weave blankets for them. Some of these "slave blankets" are now world-famous works of art.

What do we know about the Hopewell?

The Hopewell people, who once lived in the southeastern United States, have been extinct for 500 years. Little is known about their culture. But their large burial mounds have been excavated to reveal paintings that tell the stories of complicated funeral ceremonies.

Who is a famous Tlingit?

Larry McNeil is a Tlingit from Alaska, famous for his photography and his work as a professor at the Institute of American Indian Arts in Santa Fé. He became a photographer after realizing that Alaskan Native Americans were not fairly represented in art.

What are totem poles?

NATIVE AMERICANS OF THE NORTHWEST, LIKE the Haida, built totem poles as tall as 40 ft (12 m) outside their homes to advertise their family's status. The pole would usually be in the image of animals or birds that had a special meaning for the family clan and its ancestors. Each family had its own symbols and designs, and these were painted or etched onto the wooden totem pole. Totem poles were also erected as a memorial to a deceased ancestor.

Who were the greatest tattooists?

Without a doubt, they were the Timucua people of Florida. The Timucua wore little clothing because of the hot climate. This allowed them to tattoo amazingly complicated patterns over most of their bodies. Both men and woman liked to decorate their bodies with tattoos. The Mojave people of northern California specialized in facial tattooing to show their family status, while Osage women liked tattooing spiders on the backs of their hands. People on the northwest coast used tattooing to record their family's history.

Christians mistakenly thought that totem poles were statues to gods.

Government forces were sometimes defeated by Native Americans.

How could a warrior achieve great honor?

Warriors of most Plains tribes thought that being able to touch an enemy during a raid, without being touched in return, was a great honor. This act, known as a coup, was regarded more highly than actually injuring the enemy or even being able to steal their horses. Some warriors went to battle carrying a "coup stick" solely for this purpose. The Blackfeet preferred to try and capture an enemy shield.

What happened at the Little Big Horn?

The U.S. Army was defeated by a combined force of Lakota (Sioux), Cheyenne, and Arapaho warriors. The Native Americans were resisting government demands to move to reservations. The army planned to block off possible escape routes and divided its regiment into groups. The main group attacked a camp near the Little Big Horn River in June, 1876, without waiting for reinforcements that were on their way. Within an hour all 225 soldiers were wiped out.

Many Native American women were sharp shooters and able horsewomen.

Which tribes were almost wiped out by Kit Carson?

The Mescaleros, and then the Navajo, were attacked and rounded up by Colonel Kit Carson in the 1860s, during the Civil War. Those who were not killed were forced onto poor reservations where almost all of them died.

What weapons did Plains warriors carry?

WHEN THEY WENT ON A RAID, THEY TOOK BOWS, ARROWS, A lance, and a shield to protect them from the lances and arrows of the enemy. They might also carry a club with a sharpened stone or a spike at the end, and a sharp knife.

Who did the Native Americans call Long Hair?

Long Hair was General Custer, the officer in charge of the U.S. Army at the battle of the Little Big Horn. The name came from Custer's habit of letting his gold-colored hair grow long—though shortly before the battle he had it cut much shorter.

Were there any women warriors?

THERE CERTAINLY WERE! RUNNING EAGLE WAS A FAMOUS Blackfeet warrior woman who led others into battle. Buffalo Calf Road Woman was equally renowned among the Cheyenne. The Lakota (Sioux) and Crow also had a tradition of including female warriors in their raiding parties.

Who was the War Woman?

The Cherokee did not go to war without first holding a special meeting to discuss the matter. At this meeting the opinion of the community's women was represented by their spokesperson—and she was called the War Woman. The fate of captured enemies was also decided by Cherokee women.

Who said—"Always remember that your father never sold his country"?

Chief Joseph of the Nez Perce said this to his sons shortly before he died in 1871. A treaty robbing the tribe of their best land had been forced on his people. Chief Joseph wanted his children to know that he had never agreed to it. After his death, war broke out between the Nez Perce and government troops.

A warrior's weapons and battle regalia.

7,000 soldiers forced the Cherokee nation to march on the Trail of Tears.

Where was the Trail of Tears?

IT STARTED IN GEORGIA AND ENDED IN OKLAHOMA. THE DISCOVERY OF GOLD in Georgia made the presence of Native Americans there unwelcome to the whites. In 1938, some 16,000 Cherokees were rounded up by the army and forced at the point of bayonets to trek west to new land. The trek, which lasted throughout a cold winter and covered over 4,000 miles (6,700 km), became known as the Trail of Tears. When it was over, a quarter of the Cherokee nation was dead.

Whose hearts were buried at Wounded Knee?

Men, women, and children of the Lakota (Sioux) were massacred in 1890 at Wounded Knee Creek near Pine Ridge, South Dakota. It happened after a Ghost Dance (a ritual dance wishing back the good days before the whites came) when the Lakota people who surrendered were rounded up by the army. A tense situation developed and shooting broke out. A famous book about the event is entitled *Bury My Heart At Wounded Knee*.

Which state declared that the Cherokee nation did not exist?

The state of Georgia. Georgia declared Cherokees did not exist so it could forbid them from digging for gold, which had been discovered there. Georgia also made it illegal for Native Americans to testify in court, as they were not Christians.

Who was captured only 30 miles from safety?

In an attempt to escape the U.S. Army in 1877, two Native American chiefs led their people on a 1,600-mile- (2, 600 km-) trek across Idaho, Wyoming and Montana. They were Young Chief Joseph and Chief Looking Glass. They and their people were captured just before reaching safety in Canada.

Who was captured dishonorably but died honorably?

Osceola, a chief of the Seminoles in Florida, was tricked by a false flag of truce and captured. In a prison bed, he dressed in his war outfit for the last time, said farewell to the army officers and his own family, and died peacefully.

Who died while his arms were held by a fellow Native American?
Crazy Horse, who had the greatest military record of any Sioux fighting the white man, was feared by the U.S. Army, and envied by other chiefs. Arrested at the age of 37, he was bayoneted to death by a soldier, while his arms were held by the traitor Little Big Man.

Native Americans fought hard to save their way of life and traditions.

Who were the last Native Americans to fight a sustained war against the U.S. Army?
The Apaches in the 1870s. They were eventually forced onto a reservation in Arizona, but armed rebellions continued until 1896. Warriors taken in the last rebellion were finally released from prison in 1913. Where they settled, the town of Apache still stands.

Who was kidnapped and brought up as a Comanche?
The mother of Quannah Parker, a leader of the Comanches, was captured as a child from a settler's community and grew up as a Comanche. She was later recaptured and returned to her white family, but she was never able to successfully adapt to their way of life.

What did Young Chief Joseph say when his people were surrounded and outnumbered by the army?
He said these famous words—"I want to have time to look for my children and see how many I can find. Maybe I shall find them among the dead. Hear me, my chiefs, I am tired; My heart is sick and sad. From where the Sun now stands, I will fight no more forever."

How did smallpox affect the Mandans?

T HE MANDAN PEOPLE LIVED ON THE UPPER Missouri in North Dakota. When they first came into contact with European settlers and traders, they caught smallpox from them. They had no resistance to it, and it wiped them out—by 1837 fewer than 130 Mandan were still alive.

Caitlin painted 470 full length paintings of Native Americans.

Who painted Native American chiefs?

GEORGE CATLIN (1796—1872) WAS A PAINTER WHO TRAVELED WEST in the 1800s. He painted unique portraits of chiefs and Native American life, including hunting for buffalo and moose. His paintings of chiefs like Osceola are world-famous.

How did Washakie help the U.S. Army?

Washakie was a Shoshone who helped establish a successful reservation for his people. Trusted by the white authorities, he encouraged the Shoshone to act as scouts for the U.S. Army. The army honored him by renaming one of their forts in Wyoming Fort Washakie.

What was Pocahontas famous for?

She was famous for pleading for the life of Captain John Smith, an English settler in Virginia captured by the Powhatan people in 1607. She was later kidnapped by the English herself, and adapted happily to a new way of life.

Who was Sarah Winnemucca?

She was a Paiute woman, born in 1844, who learned to read and write and educated herself. She became a translator and a go-between for her own people and the government. She later wrote her own life story, telling how white people changed the Paiute way of life.

Who was the greatest Apache warrior?

Geronimo, whose first wife and three children were murdered by Mexicans, was the greatest Apache leader. Born in 1829, he led the fight against invaders of Apache land in the 1860s. He was only once caught, and that was by a trick. He boasted famously to the army—"You have never caught me shooting." He escaped captivity, but finally surrendered in 1886 and died in prison in 1909.

What did Sequoyah invent?

A written language for his Cherokee people. Sequoyah (1770—1843) realized that a written constitution and permanent records would help strengthen the position of the Cherokee people. The first Native American newspaper appeared in Cherokee in 1828.

Who was Cochise?

He was a famous and fierce chief of the Chirricahuas, an Apache tribe, who made peace with General Howard of the U.S. Army after Howard went unarmed into his camp. He stayed loyal to the terms of the treaty until he died three years later in 1874.

Did Hiawatha really exist?

YES, HE WAS A MOHAWK WHO SUPPORTED THE FORMATION OF THE IROQUOIS

Confederacy. This union of five tribes into one democratic body was the idea of the spiritual leader Deganawidah. Hiawatha was made famous in Longfellow's poem named after him

Did Sitting Bull defeat Custer?

No, Chief Sitting Bull was not even present at the battle. Battle honours belong to Gall, the Hunkpapa Sioux leader, and to Chief Crazy Horse. Sitting Bull helped to unite the tribes who fought in the battle against the army's determination to move them off their land and onto reservations. He led his people to safety in Canada when the battle was over, but the shortage of buffalo there meant they had little to eat, and in 1881 he surrendered at Fort Buford in Montana.

The battle at Little Bighorn, June 26, 1876.

Today, the Apache way of life continues in places like Arizona.

When did a president visit a Native American reservation?

In July, 1999, President Clinton paid a visit to the Pine Ridge Reservation in South Dakota, scene of the Wounded Knee massacre in 1890. It was the first visit by a U.S. president for 60 years.

Where can you visit the Cherokee Heritage Center?
Just outside Tahlequah in Oklahoma. Here, visitors can learn about the history and culture of the Cherokee nation, including the Trail of Tears and Sequoyah's invention of written Cherokee.

What are the words of a modern Pueblo prayer?
Hold onto what is good, even if it is a handful of earth.
Hold onto what you believe, even if it is a tree that stands alone.
Hold onto what you must do, even if it is a long way from home.

Are Native Americans becoming extinct?
Not at all, though it was once thought they would become extinct or simply marry into the rest of the United States. But did you know that Native Americans form only 1% of the U.S. population? They occupy more space in the imagination of the United States than they do land! In the 1970s, they went to court and settled important claims to do with territory. Today, their cultural traditions are stronger than at any time in the last 100 years.

Who helped build the Empire State Building?
Mohawks. It all goes back to the 1880s, when a dozen Mohawks were hired to work on the steel girders being erected to support tall buildings. By the 1930s, when many skyscrapers were being built in New York, Mohawk construction workers were well-known for their fearless ability to work at heights. The Empire State is just one of the structures they helped to build. The Mohawk tradition of high-rise building is still alive today.

Where can the "Lost Colony" be found?

In North Carolina, where a settlement was founded in the 1580s. Settlers moved in, but their supply ship was unable to return for three years, by which time the colony had vanished. A local tribe took pity on the settlers and let them live with them. Their descendants are the Lumbee people, who still live in North Carolina today.

Who never surrendered, but made peace in 1962?

The Mikasukis people fled to the swamplands of Florida over 150 years ago. From there, they continued to insist that they were at war with the United States and its army. Finally, in 1962, they signed a peace treaty.

What happened at Wounded Knee in 1973?

The American Indian Movement seized armed control of Wounded Knee for 71 days in protest against a history of ill-treatment by the whites. The leader of the protest movement later played a role in the 1992 film *The Last of the Mohicans*.

What is a Peacemaker's Court?

It is a modern revival of traditional Navajo justice. It was started in 1990, and operates in seven courtrooms in Navajo communities. Peacemakers, not judges, listen to a dispute and decide on compensation that will satisfy both sides in the argument.

Traditions such as the Pueblo Indians' Turkey Dance still live on.

Do pow-wows still happen?

POW-WOWS FIRST started among Plains people, but have now spread to the Southwest as well— they are definitely not a thing of the past. Over 1,000 pow-wows took place every year in the 1990s—they are social festivals celebrating a vibrant cultural life.

Pilgrims

This Iroquois warrior carries a ball-headed club as part of his ceremonial war dress.

Who was there, before the Pilgrims came?

The Algonquin and the Iroquois were native American tribes who lived in northeastern

America. The Algonquin tribes spoke the Algonquian language and they included the Abenaki, Mahican, Narragansett, Pequot, and Wampanoag. They lived mainly along the coast. The Iroquois tribes spoke the Iroquoian language. They were based inland from the Algonquin tribes—around the St. Lawrence valley and the Great Lakes.

The beads that made up a wampum belt were also a form of currency.

What is a wampum?

A WAMPUM IS A BELT OF STRUNG BEADS MADE FROM WHELK AND CLAM shells. Wampum belts were valuable and sacred objects. They were exchanged as pledges of honor in political agreements between tribes. They were also worn at important occasions, such as weddings.

Who spoke of moccasins and tomahawks?

When Europeans started to settle in northeastern America, they soon came into contact with the local peoples and learned how to communicate with them. Some words of the Algonquian language eventually became so familiar that today they are part of the English language. They include "moccasin," "moose," and "tomahawk."

What was a sachem?

Sachem was the name given by tribes of the Northeast to their leaders. The five tribes of the Iroquois League elected 50 sachems who formed the governing body of the League.

Who were the people of the longhouse?

By the early 1600s, five of the Iroquoian-speaking tribes—the Cayuga, Mohawk, Oneida, Onondoga, and Seneca—had joined together to form the Iroquois League. They called themselves the "people of the longhouse." The League was a powerful alliance in warfare, and defeated the Huron, another Iroquoian-speaking tribe, in 1649.

Who shaved their heads?

In the Northeast, Native American men often shaved most of the hair off their heads, leaving only a small tuft on top. Another style was to shave only one side of the head, painting the shaven side. Women grew their hair to full length and wore it in single or double plaits down the back.

Who lived in wigwams?

Many of the tribes in the Northeast lived in cone- or dome-shaped tepees, often covered with birchbark. But the Iroquois made large rectangular homes called longhouses. They were built of elm poles covered with bark, and they could be up to 32 ft (10 m) long. Several related families lived in a longhouse, each family with its own sleeping area. An Iroquois village usually had several longhouses, surrounded by a tall fence, named a palisade, for security.

How did they catch fish?

The Native Americans of the Northeast ate a lot of fish, which they caught off the coast and in rivers and lakes. They made small fishing boats from hollowed-out tree trunks, or canoes from birch frames covered in bark. To trap fish, they used nets, spears, and fishing lines with bone hooks.

Who grew squashes and sunflowers?

Tribes of the Northeast cleared small areas of land to grow crops such as corn, squashes, sunflowers, and beans. Corn was a very important food, eaten all year round. The women planted and looked after the crops, and gathered nuts and berries from the forest.

What did John White draw?

ONE OF THE MEMBERS OF THE EXPEDITION TO ROANOKE ISLAND in 1585 was an artist named John White. He made lots of sketches and watercolors of the animals and plants that he saw there, as well as the Native Americans he met.

What riches did Cabot find by the basketful?

Cabot did not bring back exotic spices and fabulous jewels from his voyage of 1497. But he did bring news of waters teeming with fish off the coast of Newfoundland—there were so many fish in the sea that they could be caught by lowering baskets weighted with stones over the side of the ship. Soon, fishermen from England, France, Italy, Portugal, and Spain were visiting these waters and coming home with huge loads of fish.

John White's illustrations showed what Native American life was like in the 1500s.

Who "found" Newfoundland?

The first known voyage across the Atlantic Ocean from Europe to North America was made by an Italian sailor called John Cabot in 1497. His ship was the *Matthew*, and his voyage was paid for by the English king, Henry VII. Like Christopher Columbus before him, Cabot thought that he was sailing to Asia —the land of spices and riches. Cabot did not find any riches, but he did make a landing, probably somewhere in present-day Newfoundland. Nearly a century later, in 1583, Sir Humphrey Gilbert sailed across the Atlantic on behalf of Queen Elizabeth I and claimed Newfoundland as an English territory.

Who were the first settlers to spend a winter in the New World?

In April 1585, a small fleet of five large and two smaller ships left England under the command of Richard Grenville. This expedition had been organized by Sir Walter Raleigh. Its aim was to set up a base for English warships at Roanoke Island (in present-day North Carolina). But the waters around the island were found to be too shallow for warships and, after one winter on the island, the colonists returned to England.

The Iroquois were based around the Great Lakes and lived in longhouses like these.

What was the message carved on the tree?

WHEN JOHN WHITE ARRIVED ON ROANOKE ISLAND IN 1590 TO LOOK FOR the colonists, the only clue he found was the word CROATOAN carved on a post. The Croatoan were Native Americans known to be friendly toward European settlers. They lived on a neighboring island. But storms stopped White from getting to their island, and the fate of the missing settlers was never known.

What happened to the "Lost Colony"?

In 1587, Sir Walter Raleigh organized a second expedition of colonists. This settlement was supposed to be on the mainland in the Chesapeake area—but the crossing took longer than expected and the captain refused to sail farther than Roanoke Island, where the colonists landed. The war between England and Spain and the Spanish Armada (1588) prevented any further voyages until 1590, when the artist John White sailed once again to Roanoke to join the colonists. But they had disappeared, and no trace of them was ever found.

What did the fishermen bring back apart from fish?

As the fishermen working along the coast of North America met up with the local peoples, a new trade began to develop. The Native Americans gave the fishermen furs to take back to Europe, in exchange for glass beads, cloth for clothes, and blankets, and iron tools.

Where did Jacques Cartier sail to?

Jacques Cartier was a sailor who came from St. Malo in France. Backed by the French king, Francis I, he made two expeditions in 1534 and 1535. He explored the Gulf of St Lawrence and the St. Lawrence River as far as modern-day Montreal.

Who founded Quebec?

In 1608, a group of French explorers led by Samuel de Champlain sailed to North America and made their way up the St. Lawrence River. They set up a fur trading post and named it Quebec. Only eight of the 24 colonists who founded Quebec were alive after the first winter in the new settlement, but Quebec itself survived and became the first settlement of New France.

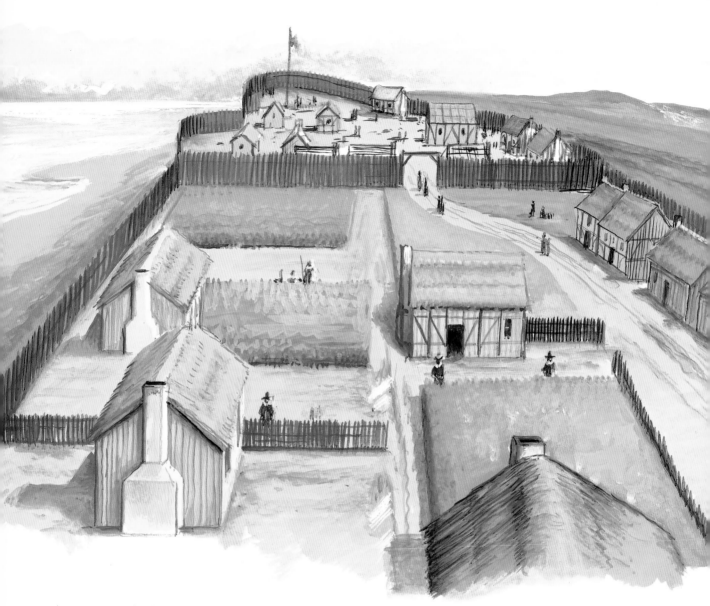

Jamestown was the site of the first
successful British settlement in America.

Why was food scarce?

THE JAMESTOWN SETTLERS OFTEN
ARGUED AMONG THEMSELVES ABOUT
the running of the colony. As the first winter drew in,
they realized that they had not grown enough crops
to eat. This was mainly because so many men had
deserted the fields to look for gold. The colony
would not have survived its first winter without food
from the Powhatans.

What treasure did English adventurers hope to find in the New World?

Gold! In the reign of Queen
Elizabeth I, many great English
captains roamed the seas. Sir
Francis Drake was the first
Englishman to sail around the
world. Sir Walter Raleigh was the
first to organize colonies of
settlers in America. These captains
were privateers—with the
permission of their queen, they
attacked and looted enemy ships,
returning in triumph with their
plunder. They also returned with
wild tales of untold riches and of
a city dripping with gold—El
Dorado. These stories inspired
many adventurers to try their luck
in the New World.

Where did three ships find a permanent home?

After a journey across the Atlantic Ocean lasting about four months, 105 men in three ships sailed up the James River in Virginia and looked for somewhere to land. The year was 1607. Their ships were owned by the London Company, and their task was to find a natural harbor that would be safe from attack by England's enemy, the Spanish. When they found a good place, the adventurers began building simple shelters there. They called their new settlement Jamestown. It was the first permanent English settlement in North America.

Who were the Jamestown adventurers?

The men who sailed across the ocean to settle Jamestown were a mixed bunch. They included soldiers, labourers, craftsmen, a doctor, a priest, and several well-off gentlemen. Most hoped to make their fortunes in the New World, and they started to explore the area, searching for gold and other treasure.

How many settlers survived the first winter?

Out of the 105 settlers who landed in April 1607, only 35 were still alive after the first winter in the colony. Many died from diseases such as typhoid, malaria, and dysentery, others from starvation. Only the arrival of more settlers in 1608 and 1609 saved the colony from dying out.

Did the Native Americans help the settlers?

The Native Americans of the area were Algonquian-speakers led by a chief named Powhatan. At first the Powhatans were suspicious, but they were soon helping the settlers with supplies of food. Later, when the Powhatans realized that the newcomers intended to stay and take over their land, they attacked the colony, burning crops and killing livestock.

Who was John Smith?

After the disastrous first winter, it took a strong man to pull the colony through the following year. This man was a soldier named John Smith. He ruled with an iron fist, forcing the settlers to plant crops, and build houses and defenses.

Why did the settlers grow tobacco?

The colonists did not find gold, but they did discover a crop that grew well in Virginia, which they could sell in England for a profit. This crop was tobacco. In 1612 a settler called John Rolfe brought the first tobacco plants from the Caribbean, and two years later the first shipload of leaves was sent back to England from America.

Ætatis suæ 21. Aº. 1616.

Pocahontas became a Christian and changed her name to Rebecca when she married John Rolfe.

What happened to Pocahontas?

In 1613, one of the daughters of Chief Powhatan, named Pocahontas, was kidnapped by the colonists. While she was held captive, Pocahontas and the tobacco farmer John Rolfe fell in love, and the pair got married. This was the first marriage between a settler and a Native American, and it helped to make relations between the two sides more friendly.

Pilgrims believed that devotion to God could only be shown through worship, not through the clothes they wore. Pilgrims dressed very simply.

Who were the Pilgrims?
In November 1620, a group of men, women, and children made landfall on the rocky coastline of New England. Like the first settlers of Jamestown, these people had come to start a new life in the New World—but the reasons for their voyage were very different. They were not searching for gold, but for the freedom to follow their religion without persecution. They were called the Pilgrim Fathers.

What was a Nonconformist?
In the late 1500s and early 1600s, some people broke away from the Catholic and Anglican Churches. Because they did not conform to the established religions, they were called Nonconformists. They did not like the pomp and ceremony of church services, and did not believe that you needed a priest to help you talk to God. Instead, they worshipped solemnly in simple surroundings. There were many different Nonconformist groups, including the Pilgrims, the Puritans, and the Separatists.

What is Scrooby?
Scrooby, a small village in Nottinghamshire, England, was the center of the Nonconformist Church of the Pilgrims. Several Pilgrim leaders came from Scrooby, including John Robinson, William Brewster, and William Bradford.

How were Pilgrim children different?

THE PILGRIMS DISAPPROVED OF THE RELAXED WAY DUTCH CHILDREN WERE BROUGHT UP. DUTCH CHILDREN HAD FREEDOM to play, but the children of Pilgrim families were treated very strictly. They had to dress in dull clothes, and generally be seen and not heard.

Why did the Pilgrims flee to the Netherlands?

I N 1608, A GROUP OF NONCONFORMISTS FLED TO THE NETHERLANDS TO ESCAPE persecution in England. This was a risky business because the punishment for illegal emigration was prison. But the reward once they reached the Netherlands was great—freedom to worship as they wanted.

Why did the women and children get left behind?
The first attempt by the Pilgrims to flee to the Netherlands was led by William Brewster and John Robinson, in 1607. But the Pilgrims were robbed by the unscrupulous captain of the ship. A year later they tried again. This time the men went aboard the ship to check that there was no trap—only to watch their women and children being rounded up by the authorities on shore. The men had to sail without their families, and it was many months before they were reunited in the Netherlands.

Many Pilgrim women were expert weavers.

Why did the Pilgrims become weavers?
At first, the Pilgrims lived in the capital of the Netherlands, Amsterdam. But after a short time, they moved to the university town of Leiden, where many of them got jobs as weavers.

What was the Pilgrim Press?
It was a printing machine set up in Leiden by William Brewster. It was used to print pamphlets about the Nonconformist Church. These pamphlets were distributed in the Netherlands and, illegally, in England.

Why did the Pilgrims decide to leave the Netherlands?
The Pilgrims did not feel at home in the Netherlands. They did not want to follow a Dutch way of life or learn the Dutch language. Many Pilgrims began to talk about going to America—carving out a new life in an entirely new land.

How many people sailed on the Mayflower?

THE SECOND SHIP THAT THE PILGRIMS CHOSE FOR THEIR VOYAGE TO THE NEW World was called the *Mayflower*. In 1620, it sailed from London to Southhampton, where it met up with the *Speedwell*. The two ships set sail together for the New World in August 1620, but were forced to turn back because the *Speedwell* was leaking very badly. A second attempt also failed, and the ships were forced to dock in Plymouth. The Pilgrims decided to abandon the *Speedwell*, and they all crowded onto the *Mayflower*. The *Mayflower* left Plymouth, England, on September 6, 1620.

Did the *Speedwell* speed well?

No! Once the Pilgrims had decided to sail across the Atlantic Ocean to the New World, their leaders looked for a ship to carry them from the Netherlands to England, and from there to their new home. They bought a small ship called the *Speedwell*, and had it fitted out to carry as many people as possible. The *Speedwell* made the short voyage to England without mishap, but it soon became clear that it was dangerously unseaworthy.

Was the crossing a good one?

No! It took 64 days from when the *Mayflower* sailed out of Plymouth harbor in England until land was sighted in the New World. The voyage was rough and stormy, and at one point it looked as if the ship might break apart. The wretched Pilgrims were thrown about helplessly in their cramped quarters, and many were continually seasick.

This illustration shows a reconstruction of the *Mayflower* in full sail.

What did the Pilgrims take with them?

The Pilgrims were going to start a new life in the New World, so they packed as much as they could into the *Mayflower's* bursting holds. They took tools and equipment, as well as seeds and livestock. Many families took their dogs. They also needed to provide for themselves while at sea, so each family had its own bedding and cooking equipment.

Who kept a journal of the voyage?

One of the organizers of the expedition to the New World was a man named William Bradford. He wrote a journal recording the adventures of the Pilgrims on the crossing. He also listed every man, woman, and child aboard the *Mayflower*. From his list we know that there were 24 households as well as some single men. Bradford later became governor of the Pilgrims' new settlement.

The *Mayflower* was a three-masted carrack ship.

How big was the Mayflower?

THE *MAYFLOWER* WAS A SMALL SHIP TO FACE THE DANGERS OF AN ATLANTIC crossing. It was about 29 ft (9m) long, with a weight of about 180 tons. With 102 passengers aboard, as well as the ship's crew, and all their belongings, conditions were extremely cramped.

Why could the Pilgrims not land when they reached the shore?

When the excited Pilgrims saw land, they were desperate to get out of their damp and dirty quarters and onto dry land. But it was many days before the ship's captain could find a safe place to drop anchor. The Pilgrims first set foot in America at Cape Cod, in what is today Provincetown, Massachusetts.

What happened to the *Mayflower*?

The master of the *Mayflower*, Captain Jones, and his crew spent the first winter in the Pilgrims' new colony. It was not until the following April (1621) that the *Mayflower* set off on its return journey to England. It reached London in May, bringing the first news of the Pilgrims' safe arrival to friends and relations back home.

What other names were given to the Pilgrim Fathers?

The people who arrived in America on the *Mayflower* are also known as the "Forefathers," the "First Comers," and the "Old Stock."

How did a shallop help find a place to settle?

After signing the Mayflower Compact, a group of men went ashore to collect firewood and find a spring with fresh drinking water. Meanwhile, on board ship, the crew and some Pilgrims began to put together the small boat, named a shallop, that had been brought for exploring the coastline. It took many days to rebuild the shallop, but when it was ready, the Pilgrims took it in turns to set out in the shallop to look for a place to settle. They finally found somewhere with a safe harbor, several freshwater streams, and some abandoned fields. They called the place New Plymouth.

How did the Pilgrims celebrate that Christmas?

The Pilgrims arrived at their new home in the middle of winter. First they needed to build some kind of shelter so that families, stores, and equipment could be moved off the *Mayflower*. They spent Christmas Eve in prayer, but on Christmas Day it was business as usual—felling trees and cutting logs for building materials.

Why were the fields deserted?

The Pilgrims settled on a site that had been cleared and farmed by people before. But the fields were deserted. The Pilgrims learned later that an epidemic had killed most of the Native American inhabitants of this settlement, known as Patuxet, just two years earlier.

Who was the first governor of the colony?

After signing the Mayflower Compact, the Pilgrims elected a governor for their new colony. His name was John Carver, and he was so well-liked and respected that he was reelected in March 1621. Sadly, he died only a few weeks later, one of the last victims of the epidemic that claimed many Pilgrims' lives.

What argument ended in a compact?

As THE *MAYFLOWER* SAILED UP AND DOWN THE COASTLINE OF CAPE COD looking for somewhere to land, the Pilgrims on board started arguing. Some simply wanted to get off the ship, no matter where; others wanted to sail on and look for a really good landing place, close to other settlements. Some of the Pilgrims threatened to break from the group and set out alone, but in the end they agreed it would be better to stay together, and they all drew up a document laying down the laws and aims of the new colony. This document has became known as the Mayflower Compact. It was signed on board the *Mayflower* by 41 of the male Pilgrims on November 21, 1620.

How many Pilgrims survived the first winter?

After the rough ocean crossing, many of the Pilgrims were weak and in poor health when they arrived in the New World. Life was hardly any easier once they made landfall. In these appalling conditions, many of the Pilgrims fell ill, and during the first winter nearly half the group perished.

The Plymouth colony named their new settlement after the English town they sailed from.

As the pilgrims had no royal charter, they established government by signing the Mayflower Compact.

When did the Pilgrims found New Plymouth?

A SMALL EXPEDITION OF PILGRIMS DECIDED ON THE SITE OF NEW Plymouth on December 21, 1620. They returned to the *Mayflower* in the shallop with the good news, and a few days later everything was prepared for the final stage of the *Mayflower's* journey—a distance of about 24 miles (40 km).

What happened to Dorothy Bradford?

Dorothy was the wife of William Bradford, who became governor of the colony after John Carver. She was one of the many Pilgrims to die in that first harsh winter. She was swept away by a sudden wave that broke over her as she stepped from the *Mayflower* into the waiting shallop below.

Did anyone give up and go home with the *Mayflower*?

No. Amazingly, despite the hardships of the winter, the surviving Pilgrims were determined to stay in the new colony, and none returned with the *Mayflower* when it departed for England in April 1621.

Initially the pilgrims and the Native Americans shared the land in harmony.

What did Samoset tell the Pilgrims?

SAMOSET HAD SPENT SOME TIME WITH THE EUROPEANS WHO FISHED ALONG THE coast, and knew enough phrases to be able to communicate with the Pilgrims. He told them about the geography of the coast to the north of New Plymouth, and that the place where they had settled had once belonged to the Patuxet tribe.

Who surprised the Pilgrims?

All that first winter, the Pilgrims were uneasily aware of the presence of Native Americans all around them. But, beset by sickness and the need to build shelter and hunt and fish for food, the settlers had little time to build defenses against any possible attack from hostile people. Then in mid-March, as the Pilgrims were holding a meeting to discuss how to defend themselves, a Native American strode into their settlement. His name was Samoset, and he was the Sagamore (chief) of the Morattigan tribe. This was the Pilgrims' first contact with the local people of the area.

How did some stolen corn save the colony?

The small groups of Pilgrims who left the *Mayflower* to search for a suitable landing place came across many signs of the Native Americans who had lived there. They unearthed some graves, filled with precious objects, which they quickly covered over again. They also found Native American stores full of corn. The Pilgrims knew that they needed all the food they could get for the winter, so they helped themselves to as much corn as they could carry. In fact, the stolen corn provided them with seed to plant the following spring and, without it, the new colony would probably not have survived.

How did the Native Americans help the Pilgrims?

THE NATIVE AMERICANS HAD LIVED OFF THE LAND FOR MANY CENTURIES, AND they were generous with their advice to the Pilgrims. They showed them how to plant the corn they had taken from an abandoned store the previous winter, and taught them new ways of cooking, farming and fishing.

What was Squanto's story?
Another Native American who spoke English was Squanto. He was from the Patuxet tribe, but had been kidnapped by the adventurer Captain Hunt and taken to London as a slave. He had managed to escape and return home. Squanto gave invaluable help to the Pilgrims, acting as an interpreter between them and the local Native Americans.

Who drew up a peace treaty?
The most important negotiations in the early days of the colony were held between Governor John Carver and the Sagamore (chief) of the Wampanoag tribe, whose name was Massasoit. With the help of the interpreter, Squanto, Carver and Massasoit drew up a peace treaty. The Pilgrims provided meat and brandy for the chief. In return, Massasoit gave them tobacco.

What was Samoset's warning?
Samoset warned the Pilgrims to beware of the Nauset tribe, who lived to the northeast of New Plymouth. The Nausets had reason to be hostile to Europeans, for only recently an English adventurer named Thomas Hunt had kidnapped several Nausets and Patuxets and taken them off to be sold as slaves.

Without advice from the Native Americans, the settlers would not have survived.

What was a house-raising?

WHEN THEY FIRST ARRIVED IN THE NEW WORLD, THE SETTLERS BUILT SHELTERS as quickly as possible from whatever materials came to hand. These simple homes were often made from wattles (woven frames) and sticks, plastered over with mud. The roofs were thatched with grass. But once a settlement was established, the colonists started to build more permanent houses. These were made of wood, and several families would work together to help with sawing tree trunks and setting heavy timbers into the ground. "House-raising" soon became a community occasion, when the owner would provide food and drink for the other settlers who came to help.

Why were the colonists afraid of the forests?
The first settlers in the New World were amazed at the thick forest that covered much of the land. It was easy to get lost in these forests, and the colonists were always fearful of attack from hostile Native Americans. So, at first, they avoided going into the woods as much as possible. Later, they used the forests as a valuable source of timber and game.

What do we remember at Thanksgiving today?
In the U.S. and Canada, Thanksgiving is celebrated every year, to remember the Pilgrims' first harvest. In the U.S. it is celebrated on the fourth Thursday of every November; in Canada the second Monday of October.

As the settlers grew used to their surroundings, they were able to build better homes that afforded them more protection.

Who planted fish?
The early settlers noticed that near rivers or the ocean, the Native Americans would place dead fish beneath their corn plants in the spring. They realized that the fish acted as a natural fertilizer, making the corn grow strongly. So the settlers followed the Native Americans' example.

Which crops did the settlers grow?
The first settlers who came to the New World from Europe brought with them seeds of the crops they grew at home, such as wheat. But they found that one of the best crops for the soil and climate of the Northeast was the corn grown by the Native Americans, and this became an important crop for the colonists.

Was the New World a land of plenty?
Yes! There were fish in the ocean and rivers, many wild berries and plants that were good for eating, and large quantities of game such as deer, ducks, and geese. There was also shellfish, such as oysters and clams, along the seashore.

Thanksgiving began as a
celebration of the first harvest.

Who carried boats on their heads?

One of the easiest ways to get around in the New World was by water, along the great rivers that flowed into the Atlantic Ocean. The colonists copied the way the Native Americans made their canoes—from long strips of birchbark—to make light craft that could easily be carried around rapids or waterfalls.

Who ate the passenger?

The colonists were astonished by the numbers of pigeons that flew in the skies of the New World. These birds were passenger pigeons, and their huge flocks sometimes blacked out the entire sky. They were very easy to catch for food—so easy that the last passenger pigeon was killed in the 1800s and the bird is now extinct.

Who ate five deer at Thanksgiving?

IN THE AUTUMN OF 1621, THE PILGRIMS HARVESTED THEIR FIRST CROPS IN THE New World. In the spring they had planted barley, peas, and the Native American corn. The corn had grown well, although the barley and peas were less successful. The Pilgrims held a feast to give thanks for this store of food, which was enough to see them through the winter. Sagamore Massasoit and about 90 of his tribe came to share the Pilgrims' feast, bringing five deer with them. This was the first Thanksgiving.

How many more Pilgrim Fathers came to Plymouth?

IN THE YEARS THAT FOLLOWED, TWO MORE SHIPS ARRIVED WITH PILGRIM settlers from the Netherlands and England. In 1623, the *Anne* sailed into Plymouth harbor carrying about 60 Pilgrims. A few days later, a small ship called the *Little James* also arrived, for the Pilgrims to use for trade along the coast of North America. Finally, in 1630, the *Handmaid* brought another 60 Pilgrims. These were the last arrivals to be able to call themselves the "Pilgrim Fathers of New England."

New arrivals landing at Plymouth without supplies placed an extra strain on already limited food supplies.

What did *Fortune* bring in 1621?
The Pilgrims had lived in the New World for one year, when an unexpected arrival took the small colony by surprise. On November 21, 1621, a ship sailed into Plymouth harbor. Fearing that it might be an enemy ship, the Pilgrims ran to grab their weapons —but it was the *Fortune* carrying a second wave of colonists. Joyfully, the Pilgrims ran to the shore to greet the new arrivals.

What good news did the *Fortune* bring?
The *Fortune* brought news and letters from friends and family at home—the first communication with the outside world since the Pilgrims had arrived in the New World.

...and what about the bad news?

The Pilgrims' expedition on the *Fortune* had been very badly planned. There was barely enough food on board to keep the new settlers alive during the crossing. To the horror of the original colonists in Plymouth, the new settlers had brought no supplies or equipment with them. The number of extra mouths to feed brought the colony close to starvation over that winter.

Who got ambushed by pirates?

The colonists loaded the *Fortune* with trade goods to be sold in England—beaver skins and roughly sawn timber. The ship set sail on December 21, 1621, but on its return journey across the Atlantic, it was captured by French pirates. They stole the Pilgrims' precious cargo and delayed the arrival of their letters in England.

Who came unprepared?

Two shiploads of adventurers from England arrived in 1622, just as the settlers were close to starvation. The new arrivals brought no supplies with them, and relied on the Pilgrims' goodwill and hospitality. When the newcomers finally left to set up their own colony, they left their sick behind for the Pilgrims to nurse back to health.

Who was brought back to life?

One day, word came to the Pilgrims that Massasoit, the Sagamore (chief) of the local Native Americans, was dying. Massasoit had been a good friend to the Pilgrims, so Governor Bradford decided to send him medicine. And after drinking the herbal remedies prepared by the Pilgrims, the Sagamore recovered.

Massasoit's statue is a tribute to the Native Americans who supported the Pilgrims during very difficult times.

What happened to the Pilgrims?

The Pilgrims survived Native American attack, starvation, and illness and their colony survived. As more settlers arrived in New England, trade increased and the Pilgrims became more prosperous. But their colony remained small and in the 1690s it was taken over by the larger and more powerful colony of Massachusetts.

What was Massasoit's warning?

To THANK THE PILGRIMS FOR THEIR HELP, MASSASOIT WARNED THEM ABOUT A planned raid. He had forbidden his own tribe to take part, but he knew that other tribes were about to attack Plymouth and a neighboring settlement set up by the English adventurers.

Like other Nonconformists, Quakers were persecuted for their beliefs.

What was the largest expedition to the New World?

In March 1630, a fleet of 11 ships left England for America. On board were nearly 1,000 men, women, and children. This massive expedition was organized by the Massachusetts Bay Company, and its leader was John Winthrop, a Puritan landowner from Suffolk in the east of England. Even before he sailed on the *Arabella*, Winthrop had been elected governor of the new colony. When they arrived in the New World, the settlers chose a site near the Charles River. They called it Boston, after the town in Lincolnshire, England, where many of them had lived.

Why did New Amsterdam become New York?

English settlers were not the only European colonizers arriving in the New World. In 1625, a small group of settlers from the Netherlands set up a trading post on Manhattan Island, calling it New Amsterdam. The colonists found that the land on Manhattan was suitable for growing crops, and the settlement flourished. Then in 1664, the Dutch colony was attacked and captured by English forces, and its name was changed—to New York, after the town of York, in England.

Were the Puritans well prepared?

Yes. The Puritan settlers had learned what to bring with them from the letters written back home by the Pilgrims. They crammed their ships full of tools and equipment, as well as livestock. Within a very short time, they had set up 11 towns around the Boston area.

How many more settlers arrived?

John Winthrop's expedition of 1630 was followed by many ships full of settlers from England. Over the next 10 years, thousands more people arrived in America to settle in New England. Many of them were Puritans, or sympathetic to the Puritan way of life.

Who were the Puritans?

THE PURITANS WERE NONCONFORMISTS WHO DISAPPROVED OF THE ANGLICAN Church. They dressed soberly in simple clothes, and they led a pure life without entertainment. In the new colonies, Governor Winthrop banned theatrical performances and drinking. But everyone had to go to church.

How many families were needed to start a town?

Towns grew up amazingly quickly as more and more settlers arrived in Massachusetts. A group of about 20 families would join together to found a new town. Once they had been granted land, they laid out a village street with a simple church at its center. A plot of land next to the church was reserved for the minister to build a house. Then areas of about one acre were marked out for the other homes.

Did everyone follow the Puritan way of life?

No! MANY SETTLERS WERE NOT PURITANS AND DID NOT LIKE THE PURITAN way of life. Some of these people formed breakaway colonies. Rhode Island was founded by Roger Williams, who had been banished from the Massachusetts colony for disagreeing with its leaders.

Who named a colony after the Virgin Mary?

The Pilgrims were not the only people to suffer religious persecution in England. When King Henry VIII set up the Anglican Church in the 1500s, Roman Catholics were prevented from worshipping as they wanted. In 1633, two ships sailed for America carrying Catholic settlers. They founded a colony and called it Maryland.

Who were the Quakers?

The Quakers were a group of English Nonconformists who followed the teaching of a preacher called George Fox. In the early 1680s, a group of Quakers organized by William Penn set sail for America. They were the first settlers in the State of Pennsylvania.

A New England kitchen contained objects brought from Europe as well as newly-crafted utensils.

Why were fish and furs important?

The early settlers discovered that their new home was rich in two valuable natural resources—fish and furs. In fact, fishermen had long known about the plentiful supplies of fish in the North Atlantic Ocean. Fur traders were often the first adventurers to explore new areas, far in advance of any settlers. Most traders bartered with the local Native Americans, who were skilled trappers, for the hides of deer, moose, bear, otter, and beaver.

What did La Salle find downriver?

After Champlain founded Quebec and New France, the land that is present-day Canada was crossed and re-crossed by adventurers in pursuit of furs. Many of these adventurers were French, and gradually they explored the area from Hudson Bay to the Great Lakes. Some pushed even farther south. From 1679 to 1682 the French explorer René Robert Cavalier de La Salle made an epic journey down the Mississippi River as far as the Gulf of Mexico, claiming a vast area of land, Louisiana, for the French crown.

Why was the Hudson's Bay Company set up?

The Hudson's Bay Company was set up in 1670 by English fur traders. English and French traders competed for control of the fur trade in the north, and quarrels often broke out between the two sides.

What was salt cod?

O F ALL THE FISH CAUGHT OFF THE COAST OF NEWFOUNDLAND, COD WAS THE MOST important. This was because it could be dried and cured with salt to stop it from going bad. The salt fish was then taken back to Europe and sold in ports such as La Rochelle on the Atlantic coast of France.

Fig. 3.

Cod fishing provided an income for many settlers.

What did the traders exchange for furs?

THE NATIVE AMERICANS PROVIDED THE VALUABLE SKINS TO THE FUR

traders in return for all sorts of goods including tools, guns, jewelry, pots, and pans, clothes, and blankets.

Furs from America fetched a good price in Europe.

Who bought the furs?
Most of the furs were shipped back to Europe. They were used for clothing—for example, deerskin was used to make gloves. Some of the furs were sold in the growing colonies along the east coast where they were used to make coats and breeches (knee-length pants).

How did the trappers get about?
Trappers usually went by canoe. Most canoes were made from birchbark. There were lots of birch trees wherever the trappers went, so repairs were quick and easy. Resin, the sticky sap from trees, was used along the canoe seams to make them watertight.

How were whales caught?
Whaling expeditions set out in small rowing boats equipped with a harpoon. A harpoon was a spear with a long line attached to it. When the boat was close enough to the whale, the harpoon was thrust deep into its body and the line let out until the injured whale was exhausted. Whaling was a very dangerous way of making a living.

How did wood produce metal?
The huge forests of northeastern America provided the settlers with a rich supply of timber for houses, shipbuilding, and barrel-making. Wood was also burned to make charcoal. The charcoal was exported to Europe, where it was used in the manufacture of iron and steel.

How did the colonists defend themselves?

ONE OF THE FIRST THINGS EUROPEAN
SETTLERS DID WHEN THEY
arrived in America was to protect themselves against possible
Native American attack. So they spent a lot of time and effort
building forts, and they set up armed forces, named militias.
Captain Miles Standish was the leader of the Pilgrims'
first militia.

Why did friendship turn to warfare?

At the start, settlers and Native Americans were often friendly to each
other. The Native Americans helped the newcomers with supplies and
know-how for their survival, as they struggled to set up their colonies. In
return, the settlers gave them goods that they did not produce for
themselves, such as pots and pans, knives, blankets, guns, and alcohol. But as
the settlers took over more land and became more threatening, the Native
Americans grew more hostile. Sometimes there was open warfare.

Who died in the massacres of 1622?

By 1622, the colony in Virginia had grown to cover an area over 100 miles
(161 km) along the James River. The local Native Americans realized that
they were losing their land and that their way of life was threatened. They
attacked the colonists and massacred over 350 settlers. Many Native
Americans died in the revenge attacks that followed.

Why did the Native Americans fall sick?

As more and more European settlers poured into America, the Native
Americans who had lived there for generations began to suffer badly, and
in many ways. Probably their worst enemy was both silent and invisible.
European settlers brought illnesses with them that were entirely new to
the Native Americans. They had no resistance to diseases such as smallpox.
Thousands of Native Americans died as epidemics swept through their
tribes in the 1600s.

As relations between
Native Americans and
settlers became strained,
armed forces were set up
in settlements.

How many died from European diseases?

It is very difficult to know exactly how many Native Americans were living in northeastern America before the arrival of the European settlers. Some historians believe that the area of New England was home to about 25,000 Native Americans in 1600. It is likely that more than half of this number died from disease in the 20 years after the first settlers arrived.

What was the Pequot War?

This was the first large-scale battle between Native Americans and settlers in the northeast. The Pequots had moved east, threatening both the local tribes and the European colonists. In 1637, the English settlers attacked the Pequots and wiped out almost the entire tribe.

Who wanted tribal warfare?

The European settlers knew that if the Native American tribes were busy fighting each other, they were less likely to attack the colonists. So, many colonies did their best to encourage bad feelings between tribes.

Who was shot in a swamp?

Chief Metacomet was finally cornered and shot in a swamp. King Philip's War was a disaster for the Native American population. Thousands died, leaving much of the coastal regions of northeast America clear for the Europeans to move into.

Who was King Philip?

After the death of Massasoit in 1662, his son Metacomet became chief. The colonists called him "Philip" or "King Philip." Because of the land they were taking from him, Metacomet was not as friendly to the settlers as his father. He led his people in a war against them that lasted from 1675 to 1676. This became known as King Philip's War.

King Philip enlisted the help of other Native American tribes in his struggle against the settlers.

Jefferson wrote part of the Declaration of Independence.

When was the Declaration of Independence?

THE AMERICAN COLONISTS DECLARED THEMSELVES INDEPENDENT FROM BRITAIN on July 4th, 1776. But the fighting went on until 1783 before Britain recognized the independence of the United States of America.

When did the first Africans arrive in North America?
Early settlers in Virginia set sail for Africa, returning with African captives to work on their plantations around 1619. This was the beginning of the terrible slave trade.

Who won the Seven Years' War?
Great Britain eventually won the war after seven long years. The capital of New France, Quebec, surrendered in 1760. By the end of the war in 1763, the British had taken over New France and governed the whole of eastern North America.

What were the 13 colonies?
Europeans continued to settle the northeast coast of America throughout the end of the 1600s and the beginning of the 1700s. By 1733, there were 13 British colonies in North America. They were Connecticut, Delaware, Georgia, Maine, Maryland, Massachusetts, New Hampshire, New Jersey, New York, Pennsylvania, Rhode Island, Vermont, and Virginia. They were all ruled by a government far away in Great Britain—but this situation was soon to change.

Who fought a war over furs?
Ever since the first trappers explored the waterways of northern America, the English and French had fought to control the fur trade, which was making them so much money. The two sides engaged in lots of small wars, often helped by their Native American allies. But the most bitter struggle began in 1754. The fighting spread to Europe in 1756, and lasted for seven years, until 1763. It became known as the Seven Years' War.

What started the American Revolution?

Which was the last of the 13 colonies to be founded?
Georgia. Its charter was issued in 1732, and the first settlers arrived from England in 1733.

D URING THE 1760S AND 1770S, THE GOVERNMENT IN BRITAIN imposed a series of taxes on the colonists in America. The colonists had no representatives in the British parliament and therefore no one to argue their cause. Finally, in 1775, the colonists' resentment boiled over into armed resistance. This was the beginning of the American Revolution.

Colonists became disillusioned with being governed by a far-off country that knew little about their lives.

Why did the British demand money from their colonies?
After the Seven Years' War the British colonists in America no longer feared a French invasion from the north. But the British government decided that their colonies needed a permanent army and navy—and they expected the colonies to pay toward the upkeep of these forces.

What happened at Bunker Hill?
The opening skirmishes of the American Revolution happened at Concord and nearby Lexington in April 1775. The first major battle was at Bunker Hill. The colonists were forced to flee, but not until they had killed or wounded more than 1,000 British soldiers.

**Who walked the
Wilderness Road?**
The trail cut across the
Appalachians by Daniel Boone
and his 30 woodsmen became
known as the Wilderness Road. It
started in Virginia, crossed the
mountains at the Cumberland
Gap, and ended in Kentucky.

Where did Daniel Boone cut a trail?

T HE SETTLERS IGNORED
THE BAN ON EXPLORING
west of the Appalachian Mountains. In
1775, a judge called Richard
Henderson bought a huge area of land
in Kentucky from the Cherokees. Then
he employed the pioneer Daniel
Boone to cut a trail through the
Appalachian Mountains to his land.
Boone had spent many years exploring
the mountains and beyond, and knew
the area better than any other white
man of the time.

Daniel Boone was captured by the
Shawnee during the American
Revolution, but escaped and reached
Boonesborough in time to save it
from the British.

Why did people go West?
To claim land. Thousands of
people from Europe continued to
pour into America. Between 1763
and 1776 alone, up to 150,000
people settled there. More people
needed more land, and the
government could do nothing to
stop them moving west to find it.

Where did Daniel Boone build a town?

At the end of the Wilderness Road, Boone and his companions built a settlement which they called Boonesborough. It was near the present-day town of Lexington. In a short time several families had settled around Boonesborough, including the owner of the territory, Judge Henderson.

Who trapped the trapper?

Boone met many Native Americans as he traveled through the mountains and beyond. Often, these meetings were hostile and Boone was taken prisoner. He was set free only after he had given up his few possessions and whatever furs he had managed to trap.

Who lost his homeland twice?

Boone lost his land in Kentucky because he could not prove his legal right to own it. In 1799, he led another group of settlers, this time into Missouri. Once again, he lost the land he had claimed. He died in Missouri in 1820.

Who drew a line at the Appalachian Mountains?

As the Seven Years' War came to an end and Britain took control of French land in North America, many Native American tribes began to rebel. These Native Americans had long been allies of the French, and they did not trust Great Britain. In 1763, after several ferocious battles between Native Americans and British troops, the British government ordered all settlers west of the Appalachian Mountains to withdraw to the east. It also forbade new settlement west of the mountains—the idea was to leave this area free for the Native Americans.

People living in frontier villages had to be entirely self-sufficient.

Who were the "back-woodsmen"?

The pioneers cleared land in the Kentucky

forests for their crops and built themselves rough houses from logs. They were known as "backwoodsmen"—farmers who needed to be entirely self-sufficient in order to survive.

Who followed Boone to the West?

For many years the Wilderness Road was the only practical route through the mountains to Kentucky. Despite its dangers, over 200,000 settlers had used the Wilderness Road to move west by 1800.

How the West was Won

Who lived in the West?

WHEN EUROPEANS FIRST ARRIVED IN THE "NEW WORLD" OF THE Americas, they did not move to an empty continent. This land had been home to millions of Native Americans for a thousand generations or more. There were over 200 different tribes in the West, speaking over 75 different languages. They included the Hopi, Clatsop, Pawnee, Mojave, Nez Perce, Shoshone, Chinook, and Zuni. Each of these peoples had their own traditions, customs and ways of life.

Who lived on the Plateau?

Bordered by the Cascade Range to the west and the Rocky Mountains to the east, the Plateau region was home to tribes such as the Chinook, the Northern Shoshone, Nez Perce, and the Kootenai. The peoples of the Plateau caught salmon in the Columbia and Fraser rivers as well as foraging for camas roots and other vegetables.

Who built houses of bark and reeds?

On the Pacific coast, the Native Americans in California built small shelters from reeds, others made tepee-like structures from the bark of the redwood tree. Further north, tribes such as the Nootka and the Haida made sturdy rectangular houses from planks of wood, tied together with cords.

What was a potlatch?

A potlatch was a ceremony held by the tribes of the Pacific Northwest such as the Tlingit and Chinook. It was a spectacular occasion when gifts were given away, people dressed in their finest clothes, and there was much feasting and celebration.

What were shells used for?

The tribes along the Pacific coast used the beautiful shells of oysters, clams and other shellfish as a kind of money. They exchanged shells for goods. Some shells ended up thousands of miles away from the coast, worn as ornaments by people who had never been anywhere near the sea.

Who lived in multi-level housing?

The peoples of the hot, dry southwest lived in settlements called pueblos. They built large living complexes out of adobe (mud brick) in which they lived all year round. The tribes of this area included the Zuni, the Acoma, and the Hopi.

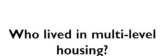

Tribes such as these Zunis were living in the West long before Europeans first arrived.

This tepee was home to a family of Crow tribespeople. The decorations on the outside show events from hunting and battles.

How was a tepee made?

A TEPEE WAS HOME FOR THE NATIVE AMERICANS OF THE GREAT Plains. It was made from a conical framework of poles covered with buffalo hides. It was ideal for the nomadic life style of the Plains peoples because it was easy to take down, easy to transport, and easy to put up again.

Where did the West begin?

As the settlers saw it, the Western frontier moved slowly westwards with them into North America. In the 1600s, the "West" was anywhere beyond the Appalachian Mountains—unknown and dangerous. By the early 1800s, European settlement had pushed westwards as far as the Mississippi, but beyond that was a wild and unfamiliar country. The expeditions of explorers such as Meriwether Lewis and William Clark, and John C. Frémont gradually opened up this wild land, and by the 1840s, pioneer families were beginning to make the long trek westwards to a new land and a new life.

Who and what lived on the Great Plains?

The Great Plains extend from the Mississippi River westwards to the Rocky Mountains. The plains were covered with endless acres of prairie grass which was home to many animals, but particularly buffalo. Tribes such as the Pawnee and Crow lived on the Great Plains, following the herds of buffalo on which they depended for their livelihoods.

These fabulous gold objects were made by the Inca people of Peru.

What strange sight did the Zunis see?

ONE DAY IN THE SUMMER OF 1540, THE ZUNI TRIBE LOOKED OUT FROM their clifftop town and saw a procession of people approaching across the desert. Most of the people were Native Americans, but there were also many paler-faced men wearing shiny metal breastplates and riding creatures never before seen by the Zunis—horses. At the head of this caravan was the Spanish conquistador (conqueror) Francisco Vásquez de Coronado.

Which animal changed the lives of the Native Americans?

Before the arrival of Europeans, Native Americans had never before seen a horse. The arrival of the horse transformed life for many Native American people. Apache and Navajo warriors were among the first to acquire horses, but herds of horses spread rapidly across the West and horses were traded from one tribe to another. Soon, horses were used for transport, for hunting buffalo, and for war.

What were the Spaniards looking for?

Gold! Coronado and the other conquistadors were searching for the "Seven Cities of Gold," great cities dripping in gold, silver, and precious jewels. Tales of such places had been brought back by conquistadors such as Alvar Núñez Cabeza de Vaca, the first European to reach the American West when he was shipwrecked there in 1528. There was also the evidence of the great riches seized from the Aztec Empire in Mexico by Hernando Cortés after 1519, and the almost unbelievable wealth plundered from the Incas in South America by Francisco Pizarro after 1532.

Did Coronado find gold?

No. Despite spending two years looking for the fabled "Seven Cities of Gold," Coronado and his expedition found only desert, endless plains, and small scruffy villages. He returned to Mexico "very sad and very weary, completely worn out...."

Coronado and his men search for the "Seven Cities of Gold."

Who went with Coronado?

The great army of people following Coronado that day in 1540 included about 300 Spanish adventurers—at least three of whom were women. There were over 1,000 Native Americans in the service of Coronado, as well as several Franciscan priests. There were also about 1,500 horses and other pack animals carrying supplies for the huge expedition.

What happened to the Zunis?

Coronado ordered the Zunis to surrender peacefully to him, but their reply was to shoot arrows and hurl stones. However, they were no match for the Spanish horses, lances, and guns, and the Zunis were quickly overpowered. The expedition took over the Zunis' settlement and stole their food—but to their disappointment the conquistadors found no gold or treasure.

What was the silent killer the Europeans brought with them?

Guns and horses may have terrified the Native Americans who first came in contact with Europeans, but the invaders carried with them a far more dangerous threat—disease. The Native Americans had no resistance to European diseases such as smallpox, cholera, measles, and tuberculosis, and sickness spread rapidly through many tribes killing millions of Native Americans.

Where was El Pueblo de Nuestra Señora la Reina de los Angeles?

Today the city with this very long name, which means "the village of our lady the queen of the angels," is better known as Los Angeles. It was founded by a group of pioneers in 1781, built in a virtual desert, but the settlers used water from the foothills of the Sierra Nevada mountains to grow crops and raise livestock.

Who was Francisco Vásquez de Coronado?

Francisco Vásquez de Coronado (1510–1554) was one of the Spanish soldiers who went to the "New World" to seek their fortunes in the 1500s.

Which Europeans first saw the Grand Canyon?

SOME MEMBERS OF CORONADO'S PARTY TRAVELED NORTHWEST from the Zuni settlements to search for treasure. Instead of precious metals and jewels they came across a gorge vast beyond their wildest dreams. They were the first Europeans to see the Grand Canyon.

Meriwether Lewis (left) and William Clark.

Who were Lewis and Clark?

M ERIWETHER LEWIS WAS THE MAN CHOSEN BY THOMAS Jefferson, third President of the United States, to lead an important expedition. Once he had been appointed, Lewis asked his friend William Clark to join him as co-leader. Together they headed a group of soldiers, explorers, and others who made up the Corps of Discovery. The task of the expedition was to travel through the territory that lay west of the Mississippi River finding out about the land, the people, the rivers—anything of interest about this vast, unknown country.

How did the Corps travel?

The Corps of Discovery set off on their journey up the Missouri River. They traveled in a large boat, called a keelboat. It was 55 ft (17 m) long, and could float in very shallow water. There were a few cabins, but most of the crew lived and slept on the open deck, covered by canvas. The keelboat could be sailed if the wind was in the right direction, rowed or towed along by human power if not. The expedition also had two large canoes, pirogues, which were each about 50 ft (15 m) long.

Why did Lewis and Clark make the incredible journey?

President Jefferson was delighted about the purchase of Louisiana, but the only problem was that he did not really know what he had bought. No one knew the exact size of Louisiana, and the only information about the land came from fur trappers. This is why Jefferson decided to send Lewis and Clark on their historic journey.

Who needed a collapsible boat?

Lewis took a collapsible boat for use later on in the expedition. He knew that the keelboat and pirogues would be left behind at some point, so he carefully designed an iron framework, which was packed into crates. Unfortunately, when the boat was eventually put together it would not float, and Lewis was forced to abandon it.

How many people were there in the Corps?

When it set off, the Corps probably numbered around 40 to 50 people, but we do not know for certain exactly how many. It included soldiers, several boatmen, a hunter named George Drouillard, and Clark's slave named York, as well as Lewis's large Newfoundland dog.

What did they take to eat?

Not much. Lewis and Clark took some provisions with them, but they were meant for emergencies only. They planned to hunt and fish for their food, and to barter with the Native Americans they met on the way.

Where did they set off from?

The Corps spent the winter in a camp just outside St Louis, where the Missouri and the Mississippi rivers meet. They set off on their famous journey on the afternoon of May 14, 1804.

Who bought Louisiana?

IN ONE OF THE BIGGEST BARGAINS IN HISTORY—THE LOUISIANA PURCHASE—

Jefferson bought a vast area of land west of the Mississippi River and north of the Gulf of Mexico. This region was called Louisiana, and Jefferson paid the French $15 million for it. This purchase in 1803 more than doubled the size of the United States.

Who took a medal of peace?

One of the aims of the expedition was to find out about the Native Americans living in the newly purchased Louisiana Territory. Lewis and Clark had strict instructions from President Jefferson to keep up good relations with the Native Americans they met on the journey. The expedition took many goods to offer as gifts to the Native Americans including beads, mirrors, combs, ribbons, cloth, knives, and fishhooks. There was also a special peace medal which showed hands clasped in friendship on one side, and President Jefferson on the other.

Lewis and Clark took presents to give to the Native Americans they met on their expedition.

Lewis and Clark by the Columbia River.

What helped the expedition?

In August 1805, the expedition entered territory under the control of the Shoshone tribe. At first the Shoshone were very suspicious of the explorers. But just when things began to look rather threatening, Sacajawea suddenly recognized the Shoshone chief – it was her brother whom she had not seen since her kidnapping! There was great rejoicing as the two were reunited.

How long were Lewis and Clark away?

The Corps of Discovery were away for nearly two and a half years and they traveled over 4,300 m (7,000 km). They sailed up the Missouri River, crossed the fearsome Rocky Mountains, and braved the rapids of the mighty Columbia River before reaching the Pacific Ocean in what is present-day Oregon. They spent the winter of 1805–1806 in Fort Clatsop on the Pacific coast. The outward journey took 18 months but the journey home took only six months! The Corps of Discovery arrived back in St Louis on September 23, 1806 to the cheers of the townspeople.

How did the expedition celebrate Christmas?

Christmas 1805 was spent in the confined quarters of Fort Clatsop. The explorers gave each other small gifts such as wool clothing, a Native American basket, a silk handkerchief, and moccasins. They celebrated with singing and dancing, and a week later greeted the New Year with a salute fired from their rifles into the air.

Who was Sacajawea?

The first winter of the expedition (1804–1805), the Corps built a fort near the villages of the Mandan tribe. During their stay at Fort Mandan, Lewis and Clark hired a French-Canadian trader called Toussaint Charbonneau and his wife Sacajawea. Their baby son, Jean Baptiste, also joined the expedition. Sacajawea was a Native American of the Shoshone tribe who had been kidnapped as a child. As a result of her local knowledge and contacts she quickly became a vital member of the Corps of Discovery.

Sacajawea, the expedition's Native American guide, points the way.

What does Nez Perce mean?

Nez perce was the name given by French traders to a native American tribe that lived in the Rocky Mountains. It means "pierced nose"—the members of this tribe wore ornaments through their noses. Nez Perce guides gave vital help to the Corps as they traveled through the mountains.

What happened at the Short and Long Narrows?

I N OCTOBER 1805, THE EXPEDITION REACHED THE MIGHTY COLUMBIA River. By this time the Corps was traveling in five dugout canoes. When the water became too rough for the canoes, the explorers had to pull them out and carry them and all their equipment to a calmer part of the river. But when they reached the Short and Long Narrows—a terrifying stretch of rapids between towering cliffs—there was little choice but to continue through the boiling waters. Despite their unwieldy canoes, the brave explorers survived—to the astonishment of the local Native Americans!

Who shot Meriwether Lewis?

One day, while out hunting, a short-sighted member of the expedition saw a movement in the grass and shot at what he thought was an elk. Unfortunately it turned out to be his commanding officer, Meriwether Lewis! Luckily the wound was not dangerous, and it healed rapidly over the next few weeks.

What animals did the expedition meet?

The members of the Corps of Discovery came across a bewildering array of wildlife during the expedition. They saw vast herds of antelope, buffalo, and elk, and described some frightening encounters with grizzly bears. They investigated the burrows of prairie dogs, watched Bighorn sheep walk across seemingly vertical cliff faces, and shot a Californian condor with a wingspan of nearly 10 ft (3 m).

Was the expedition a success?

The short answer is yes! The expedition returned safely, with the loss of only one member. Lewis and Clark made maps of the territory they crossed, and described hundreds of plants and animals previously unknown to Americans. And, as instructed by President Jefferson, the Corps struck up peaceful relations with the Native Americans they met on their journey.

Who were the mountain men?

THE MOUNTAIN MEN WERE FUR TRAPPERS. THEY CAUGHT ANIMALS SUCH AS beavers and sea otters for their pelts. These fur trappers were hard men. They frequently spent weeks alone in the mountains, traveling on foot and by canoe, camping in makeshift shelters, scavenging for food, and with only a rifle for protection against attacks from grizzly bears. Mountain men came from all backgrounds and from all over the globe: there were French, Russian, English, and American trappers as well as many Native Americans and some African Americans.

What did a mountain man wear?

Not surprisingly, many mountain men wore furs themselves. They often dressed in homemade clothes of fur and buckskin which were warm, comfortable, and easy to repair. Such clothes also provided excellent camouflage in the wild.

How did the mountain men survive the winters?

The main times for trapping were spring and autumn. The summer was the time for the annual rendezvous. Winter was spent lying low in camp, trading, mending traps, and waiting for the spring—the best time for trapping because the beavers still had their thick, luxurious winter coats.

A fur trapper heads up into the mountains. His horses are loaded with supplies to help him survive for weeks or even months.

What was a rendezvous?

Every summer, the mountain men would take their season's haul of pelts to a gathering known as a rendezvous. This was a kind of trade fair where the trappers would sell or barter their precious furs for money, supplies for the coming year and other goods. Once the serious bargaining was over, these gatherings often turned into wild parties. After the rendezvous, many trappers would return to the mountains having spent much of their year's income on drink, tobacco, and gambling!

Where did the furs go?

The beaver pelts were sent to the east coast of America and to Europe. Beaver fur was highly prized for making soft, waterproof felt, which was then used to make all sorts of hats. It was also used to trim ladies' coats and dresses. It was the height of fashion until the late 1830s, when styles in the big cities began to change and silk became all the rage. As demand fell, more and more of the mountain men found themselves out of work.

A trapper setting his beaver traps.

Who was Kit Carson?

KIT CARSON (1809–1868) WAS A FAMOUS MOUNTAIN MAN WHO WORKED IN the fur trade for over 10 years. In 1842 he was hired as a guide to the expeditions led by John C. Frémont, which explored much of Oregon and California.

What happened to the mountain men?

After the collapse of the fur trade, many mountain men were out of a job. Some returned to normal life in the east; others made use of their knowledge of the geography and ways of the West and became guides for explorers such as John C. Frémont, or for wagon trains of pioneer families.

How did Lewis and Clark help the fur trade?

After the success of the expedition of the Corps of Discovery, a New York merchant called John Jacob Astor decided to set up fur trading posts all along the route of the expedition. Astor created the American Fur Company in 1808, and the Pacific Fur Company in 1810. He founded a settlement called Astoria at the mouth of the Columbia River, near where Lewis and Clark had spent the winter in Fort Clatsop.

What replaced beaver?

Beaver fur may have gone out of fashion in the 1830s and 1840s, but there was still a demand for buffalo hide to make buffalo robes. Many Native Americans on the Great Plains, west of the Missouri River, hunted buffalo and sold their hides to organizations such as the American Fur Company.

107

A Mormon pioneer family outside their cabin in Echo City, Utah, in 1869.

What happened on June 27, 1844?

On June 27, 1844, in the town of Nauvoo, Illinois, an angry mob broke into the local jail, dragged out a man named Joseph Smith and shot him dead. Smith was the founder and leader of the Church of Jesus Christ of Latter Day Saints —the Mormons. Smith and his followers had been persecuted ever since the founding of the Mormon Church in 1830, and they had already been forced to move from New York State to Ohio, to Missouri, and then to Illinois when Smith was murdered.

Who followed Brigham Young?

AFTER SMITH'S DEATH, HIS PLACE AS LEADER OF THE MORMONS WAS taken by Brigham Young. He knew that Smith had plans to move his people once more, to the wide open spaces of the Great Basin beneath the Rocky Mountains. He decided to put this plan into action, and when the Mormons were hounded out of Nauvoo in 1846, he led about 12,000 people along the Mormon Trail, across the Mississippi River, through Iowa and Nebraska, and across the Rockies.

Why was Joseph Smith murdered?

One of the beliefs of the Mormon religion was that a man could marry more than one wife. This is known as polygamy. This practice upset people wherever the Mormons went, and led to Smith's brutal murder in Nauvoo, Illinois.

Who said "This is the place"?

In August 1847, a small party of Mormons led by Brigham Young stopped on an arid, treeless plateau. Looking around him, Young said: "This is the place." This was the Great Salt Lake valley, and it was here that the Mormons founded Salt Lake City, in present-day Utah.

How did the Mormons survive?

When the Mormons arrived in the inhospitable land chosen to be their home, they had to work extremely hard to survive. Under Young's leadership they dug irrigation channels, using water from the surrounding hills to water their crops. Fifty years later, much of the barren desert had been transformed into a fruitful land.

Who was killed in the Mountain Meadows Massacre?

Where was Deseret?
The Kingdom of Deseret, meaning "Land of the Honey Bee" was the name that the Mormons gave to their new homeland. Young wanted to extend Deseret westwards to the Pacific Ocean, but the U.S. government had other ideas. Instead, the state of Utah was created in 1850, with reduced boundaries.

IN 1857 THE MORMONS WERE ON THE LOOKOUT FOR GOVERNMENT troops. In September, a wagon train passed through Mormon territory and, convinced that it was a threat, the Mormons, helped by some Paiuté Native Americans, attacked. In fact, the wagon train was full of pioneers and over 100 of the migrants were killed.

Mormons on their long journey to Utah. They were led by Brigham Young.

What was the Utah War?
In 1852, the leaders of the Mormon Church admitted publicly for the first time that its members practised polygamy. Trouble between Mormons and nonMormons broke out, and in 1857 troops were sent to Utah. In fact, there was very little fighting in the Utah War, and it ended in 1858.

Cooking over a camp fire.

Where did the Oregon and California trails go?

In 1840, there were fewer than 150 Americans living in the vast area in the American West known as Oregon. Only five years later, there were thousands of American settlers in the region. Most had traveled across the continent of America along the 2,000-mile (3,200-km) Oregon Trail. This trail usually started in Independence, Missouri, crossed the Great Plains and the Rocky Mountains, and ended in the Columbia River region of Oregon. An alternative trail, the California Trail, followed the same route until Fort Hall, west of the Rocky Mountains, when it branched southwards, ending in the Sacramento valley.

What was a "prairie schooner"?

OVER 1,000 PEOPLE SET OFF ALONG THE OREGON TRAIL IN 1843, THE start of the "Great Migration" to the West. They traveled in heavy wooden wagons called Conestoga wagons, pulled by horses, mules, or oxen. Later pioneers along the trail used lighter wagons which were known as "prairie schooners," because their white canvas tops looked rather like the sails on a ship called a schooner. The settlers packed their belongings into the wagons, as well as supplies for the journey. Only babies and sick people actually rode in the wagons—everyone else walked.

Who wore bloomers?

Many pioneer women found that the heavy, full-length dresses that were the usual dress of the period were hopelessly impractical for life on the trail. Some women started to wear shorter dresses that did not reach all the way to the ground; others even dared to wear "bloomers"—a type of pants.

How many wagons were there in a wagon train?

Settlers traveled in groups along the trail for safety and for companionship, and there could be anything up to 100 wagons in a wagon train. The train traveled very slowly—at little over 1 mph (1.5 kph) and was on the move for nine or 10 hours every day.

A pioneer wagon loaded with a family's possessions.

Who was in charge of the train?

In the spring, groups of pioneers met in rendezvous towns such as Independence or St Joseph, Missouri or Council Bluffs, Iowa. They formed wagon-train companies and elected a leader, known as the raid captain. They also employed guides to lead them along the trail.

What happened at night?

At the end of a long day on the trail, the wagons would draw up into circles and set up camp for the night. These wagon circles gave the settlers protection in case of attack from Native Americans.

What did the men do?

The men in a wagon train were in charge of driving and repairing their wagons and looking after their livestock. They also hunted for food, and took turns standing guard at night, keeping watch for hostile Native Americans.

What were the women's jobs?

During the long, arduous journey, the women on a wagon train were in charge of preparing food—rising before dawn to ensure that a fire was lit and food was ready. They also washed and mended clothes, and looked after the children and sick people.

The Oregon Trail and the California Trail both began in Independence, Missouri.

How long was the journey?

The journey from Missouri to Oregon took about eight months, usually starting in April. It was vital to get through the coastal mountain ranges (the Cascades and the Sierra Nevada) before the winter snows set in. But starting out too early was dangerous too—settlers ran the risk that there would not be enough grass for their livestock to eat.

Why did so many pioneers die?

THOUSANDS OF PEOPLE DIED ALONG THE OREGON AND CALIFORNIA TRAILS.

One estimate is that seven people died for every mile of the route. The biggest killer was disease, particularly cholera. However, the greatest fear for the pioneers was attack from Native Americans. In fact, very few people died as a result of such attacks.

John Sutter. The California Gold Rush began when gold was found by one of his workers.

Who found gold in California?

O N A JANUARY MORNING IN 1848, A CARPENTER CALLED JAMES
Marshall was sent by his employer, John Sutter, to inspect some work on a sawmill. The mill was on a bend of the America River in California. As Marshall inspected a ditch dug out of the bed of the millstream, he noticed something glittering on the bottom. He bent down and saw several golden-yellow rocks, about the size of small peas.
Marshall had found gold!

Was it real gold?

When Marshall found the yellow rocks in the millstream he immediately rushed to find his employer, John Sutter. There was just one question on the mens' minds: Was this real gold? After trying out various tests on the precious nuggets there was no doubt. In fact, Sutter was not happy with Marshall's discovery. He did not actually own the land on which the sawmill was built, and feared that his estate would be overrun by gold-seekers—which is exactly what happened.

How do we know Marshall did find the gold?

An entry in the diary of one of the workmen working at Sutter's Mill agrees with Marshall's story of the discovery of the gold. It reads: "This day some kind of mettle [metal] was found in the tail race that looks like goald [gold]. First discovered by James Martial [Marshall], the Boss of the Mill."

How did the secret get out?

Marshall and Sutter tried to keep their discovery a secret. But, while Sutter tried unsuccessfully to claim the land on which the sawmill stood, rumor started to spread. At first, workers at the sawmill did some quiet prospecting, then their neighbors joined in, then the news began to spread further.

What did President Polk show to Congress?

At first, not everyone believed in the wild tales of gold coming from the West. Many people back East dismissed the tales as fanciful rumors. But in December 1848, President Polk showed a tea box full of gold dust to Congress—proof that the rumors were true!

Who was Sam Brannan?

STOREKEEPER SAM BRANNAN WAS DETERMINED THAT EVERYONE SHOULD know about the goldfields. In May 1848, he galloped through the streets of San Francisco waving his hat and shouting: "Gold! Gold from the America River!" Within a few weeks, three out of four men in the town had gone to look for gold.

How did Sam Brannan make his fortune?

Why was Sam Brannan so eager to spread the news about the gold? He was a clever tradesman who owned several stores selling hardware, such as picks and shovels. Brannan realized that there was a fortune to be made selling his supplies to the thousands of gold-seekers—and he did become a very rich man.

Where did the prospectors come from?

Once the news of gold reached San Francisco it traveled like wildfire—across California, north to Oregon, south as far as Peru and Chile, and across the Pacific Ocean to Hawaii. In the spring and summer of 1848, gold-seekers began to pour into the area—and it seemed that there was plenty of gold for everyone.

Which gold-finders died very poor?

Marshall and Sutter both died in poverty. Marshall spent the rest of his life wandering through the hills of California looking for more gold, but with little success. Sutter saw his estate overrun with gold-seekers, as he had predicted. After several unsuccessful prospecting ventures he moved to Pennsylvania and died, heartbroken, in 1880.

A prospector panning for gold in a stream in California.

Who were the "forty-niners"?

An early advert for Levi jeans.

ONCE PRESIDENT POLK HAD PROVED THAT THERE REALLY WAS A goldmine in the American West, the "Gold Rush" began. In 1849, about 90,000 people headed for California from all over the globe. They became known as the "forty-niners."

How did the gold seekers get to California?

There were many different routes to reach the goldfields—all dangerous. Many people walked overland—some as far as 2,000 miles (3,300 km). Others went by sea to Panama, traveled overland to the Pacific Ocean and continued to San Francisco by sea. Many died before they reached California.

A poster advertising voyages from New York to San Francisco in California. Sailing was the quickest way to get there – and the most expensive.

Who wrote: "Go West, young man, go West!"?

These words appeared in an American newspaper editorial in 1851. By that time, many thousands of hopeful gold-seekers had already headed West across the American continent in the hope of making their fortunes. Most of them were men who left behind their homes and families, intending to return after a few months or years, rich beyond their wildest dreams. Very few succeeded.

What did a shout of: "Color!" mean?

It meant that the prospectors had struck lucky and found gold. The early prospectors discovered gold quite easily on the beds of rivers and streams. They used a flat "pan" to swirl a mixture of gravel and water around until the lighter gravel was washed away, leaving the heavier gold behind. But as time went on, finding gold became harder. Prospectors had to dig deeper using long wooden boxes called cradles to sort the mud and gravel from any gold.

Where did barmen find gold?

The answer is on the floor of the bar! Many miners used pinches of gold dust to pay for refreshment, and after a long night of serving drinks, barmen in California would pan the floor of the saloon to pick up any gold that had fallen there!

What did Levi Strauss sell to the prospectors?

Levi Strauss was a German immigrant living in New York when the Gold Rush started. He traveled to the West and sold cotton material which he advertised as ideal for making tents. However, it turned out to be rather more suitable for pants— the first Levis.

Where were Lousy Ravine and Bogus Thunder?

THESE ARE BOTH NAMES OF GOLD-MINING CAMPS IN CALIFORNIA, LONG since abandoned. Names of gold camps and towns often told their own stories, such as You Bet, Git-Up-and-Git, and Bedbug!

How much did an egg cost?
When they arrived in California, prospectors were amazed at the high price of food and supplies. One egg cost as much as $3. Everything—from accommodation to picks and shovels—was overpriced, and the gold-seekers had little choice but to pay up.

What are ghost towns?
Today, you can see many reminders of the Gold Rush in the American West. The gold miners built camps and towns wherever they struck gold, and they abandoned them just as quickly when the gold ran out. Many of these towns survive as "ghost towns"—empty and in ruins.

These prospectors are using a "long tom" to search for gold. The running water separated out pieces of gold from dirt, stones and other waste.

Who built the railroad across America?

IN 1862, CONGRESS PASSED AN ACT TO AUTHORIZE THE CONSTRUCTION of a railroad (railway) that would link the east and the west coasts of America. Two companies were given the contracts to build the railroad. The Union Pacific started in Omaha, Nebraska, and worked westwards. The Central Pacific started in Sacramento, west of the Sierra Nevada mountains, and worked eastwards. Construction of the tracks started in 1863 and took over five years to complete.

What happened when the companies met?

The two bands of workers came face to face in Utah, and at first they kept building—each side refusing to stop building in the hope of getting extra pay for the extra mile or two! The government stepped in to order the line to meet at Promontory Summit—but not before a few fights had broken out between the rival workers.

The railroad linked the east and west coasts of the United States.

What happened on May 10, 1869?

In May 1869, at Promontory Summit, Utah, the tracks of the Union Pacific and the Central Pacific finally met. The Governor of California and president of the Central Pacific, Leland Stanford, lifted the hammer and brought it down to hit the last spike in the track—a golden one. He missed, but the telegraph man sent the news nevertheless: "DONE!" In Washington D.C. a great cheer greeted the news, and in San Francisco, celebrations began.

Why was it a race?

The companies were paid by the government for every mile of track they laid, between $16,000 and $48,000 per mile depending on the difficulty of the terrain. They also received land on either side of the track. Not surprisingly, construction turned into a race between the two companies to see which could lay the most track.

Who worked for the Central Pacific?

Not only did the Central Pacific company have to bring its supplies by ship around South America, it also had to drive the railroad through the Sierra Nevada mountains. To do this work, thousands of laborers were recruited in China and brought to California.

How many Chinese laborers died for the railroad?

It is estimated that over 1,000 Chinese workers died during the construction of the railroad. They struggled against appalling conditions in the Sierra Nevada mountains, blasting holes with dynamite in solid rock, working in baskets precariously slung by ropes over huge drops, and cutting down giant redwood trees.

Who won the railroad race?

The Union Pacific company laid more track than the Central Pacific —but the Union Pacific workers had an easier task. Much of the eastern part of the railroad was across the Great Plains, and they had a direct supply route from the east.

Hammering in a golden spike at the point where the Union Pacific and Central Pacific railroads met.

How was the track laid?

EVERY PART OF THE TRACK WAS LAID BY HAND. ADVANCE PARTIES LEVELED out the land ready for the heavy crossways timbers, called ties. The iron rails were laid on to the timbers and attached by spikes and bolts. Only two or three miles of track were laid per day.

What did the Native Americans think of the railroad?

The railroad cut through Native Americans' land and hunters shot thousands of buffalo to feed the hungry railroad workers. The Native Americans showed their anger by attacking the construction crews.

A pioneer farmer using a horse-drawn plow to break up the soil of the prairie.

What was a soddy?

THE FIRST TASK FOR ANY PIONEER WAS TO BUILD A SHELTER FOR

protection against the searingly hot summer sun and the icy winter blast on the prairies. The quickest way of making a shelter was to make a dugout in the side of a hill, using the excavated earth to make a wall at the front of the cave. In the spring, pioneers made houses from turf sods, known as soddies. The inside walls of these houses were lined with clay.

A pioneer family outside their sod house, or "soddy."

Why were windmills important?

Life on the Great Plains would have been impossible without windmills. Water was very scarce on the surface of the prairies, so it had to be drawn from underground wells. The constant winds turned the mills and pumped water from deep underground.

Who bought wheat with them?

In 1874, immigrants from the Crimea region of Russia brought with them a particularly hardy type of wheat, called Turkey Red. They planted it on their new farms in Kansas and it flourished. In a short time, the region had became the major wheat-producing region of the United States.

What hardships did the pioneers face?

Life on the prairies was very hard for the early pioneer farmers. Winters were bitterly cold and summers baking hot. Fire was a constant danger, as well as tornadoes, droughts and, in spring, floods. There were also plagues of insects such as grasshoppers, which got everywhere and ate everything.

Were children expected to work?

EVERYONE IN THE PIONEER FAMILY HAD TO WORK HARD SIMPLY TO SURVIVE, and children were no exception. They gathered buffalo dung for fuel, fed the animals, fetched water, and weeded vegetable gardens. During harvest, children helped their parents in the fields.

What kind of plow did the pioneers use?

The soil of the prairies was heavy and difficult to plow at first. The pioneers used a heavy steel plow that was invented by John Deere in 1837. This plow was strong enough to cut through the heavy soil and to turn it over.

Where did the pioneers come from?

Many pioneers came from Europe, drawn by the offer of free land and a chance to start afresh. They came from Norway and Russia, Scotland, France, the Netherlands and Ireland. Some English pioneers bought land in Kansas, but after a few years most of them had returned home.

What was barbed wire used for?

There were few trees on the prairies, so wood was very scarce. Without wood, the pioneers planted prickly hedges to fence off their farmland. But the invention of barbed wire in the early 1870s made fencing much better.

A cowboy trail boss in Montana, 1888.

What was a trail drive?

Trail drives started in the south, in Texas near the Gulf of Mexico. Two or three thousand cattle were rounded up and then driven day after day, week after week, northwards to the nearest railroad junction. The first of these railroad links was Abilene in Kansas. The trail drive from Texas to Abilene took about three months and it became known as the Chisholm Trail. The earliest trail drives were in 1867, when an estimated 35,000 cattle made the journey along the Chisholm Trail.

What was life like on a trail drive?

Trail drives lasted three or four months and, at first, the cowboys had to live on what they could carry and cook for themselves. They ate mostly beans and hard bread. Later, when trail drives became more organized, a chuck wagon accompanied the cowboys carrying food, water and other supplies.

What was a ranch?

As the cattle business boomed, some Texas cattlemen set up large farms, known as ranches. The ranch owner employed cowboys to work full-time looking after his cattle. The owner lived in a house in the center of the ranch; the cowboys often lived in bunkhouses.

Why did the cattle move so slowly?

On the trail, it was important not to drive the cattle too hard. They needed to arrive at the railhead in good condition. On the journey, the cattle grazed on the grass that was freely available across the Great Plains. As well as the Chisholm, there were several other trails including the Shawnee, the Western and the Goodnight-Loving Trail.

What was a bronco?

ONE OF A COWBOY'S JOBS ON THE RANCH WAS TO BREAK IN untamed horses, called broncos. A wild horse was caught with a lassoo. It was then up to the cowboy to blindfold and saddle the horse before getting into the saddle. The horse would then start bucking and rearing, trying to throw the cowboy from its back. Many cowboys were injured trying to tame broncos.

Who was Joseph G. McCoy?

It is claimed that McCoy was the first person to organize a trail drive. He recruited experienced cowboys from Texas to drive the herds northwards. In Texas the cattle would fetch no more than $4 a head: in Kansas the price was nearer $40!

What did cowboys wear?

HIGH-HEELED BOOTS,

leather "chaps" for the legs, wide-brimmed Stetson hat, a lassoo, and a cowboy saddle were the distinctive trademarks of a cowboy. The cattle business had long been established in Mexico and the southern United States, but the arrival of the railroads saw the beginning of a new era. Now, cattle could be driven across the Great Plains to the nearest railroad link, then transported to markets in the east and the north where they fetched high prices. And with the cattle came the cowboys.

Why were cattle branded?
So that they could identify which cattle belonged to which ranch, they were branded. This involved burning a special mark into the hide of the cow with a hot metal iron. Every ranch had its own identifying mark. An unmarked cow was known as a maverick.

A cowboy in his working clothes.

How old were cowboys?
The average age of a cowboy was 24. Many cowboys were Mexicans, or African Americans, and most earned no more than $30 a month. Their lives were incredibly tough. They owned their clothes, precious saddles, and guns but little else, although a few also had their own horses.

Who was Billy the Kid?

A NOTORIOUS OUTLAW, BILLY THE KID WAS SAID TO HAVE KILLED 27 people before his early death at the age of 21. It is hard to know who he was—in his early years he went by the name of Henry McCarty; Later he called himself William H. Bonney Jr.

How did bandits hold up a train?

One classic Wild West method was to wait until night, then signal with a red lantern for the chosen train to stop. The outlaws often took over the train, driving it to a safe spot before using dynamite to open the safe where the money was stored. The explosion could blow banknotes far and wide, which the bandits would quickly collect before disappearing into the night.

Who carried out the first train robberies?

In October 1866, members of the Reno Gang held up a train on the Ohio and Mississippi Railroad, stealing more than $13,000. The Reno gang was just one of the many gangs of bandits and outlaws that terrorized the West during the pioneer years, robbing banks, stagecoaches, and trains, and stealing horses and cattle.

This Colt revolver was owned by the outlaw Jesse James.

What was the Hole-in-the-Wall?

The Hole-in-the-Wall was the name of a gorge that was home to 100 or more bandits in the 1890s. It lay about 50 m (81 km) south of Buffalo, in Wyoming. Most of the outlaws were cattle or horse thieves. They were known as the "Wild Bunch," and its most famous members were Butch Cassidy and the Sundance Kid.

Why was Belle Starr called the "Bandit Queen"?

Women, as well as men, turned to violence as a way of life in the Wild West. One of the most famous female bandits was Belle Starr. Her skill on horseback, armed with a brace of pistols, earned her the title the "Bandit Queen."

What happened in Northfield, Minnesota in 1876?

On September 7, 1876, the infamous James-Younger Gang, led by brothers Jesse and Frank James, held up the First National Bank of Northfield. But the cashier refused to open the vault where the money was kept, and the townspeople started to fire at the robbers. After a desperate battle the gang escaped—but many of its members were killed or injured.

What happened at the O.K. Corral?

The infamous Jesse James posed for this photograph in 1864. At that time, he was fighting in the American Civil War.

IN 1881, THERE WAS A FAMOUS GUNFIGHT AT THE O.K. Corral in Tombstone, Arizona—the result of a feud between rival gangs in the town. Involved in the fight was Wyatt Earp. He was in fact a lawman, serving as a deputy sheriff and as a U.S. marshal, but his history was as violent and colorful as that of many criminals.

The Reno Gang prepare to rob a train on the move.

Was Jesse James a hero?

Many myths and romantic stories grew up about the outlaws of the Wild West. The bandit, Jesse James, was often portrayed as a Robin Hood figure who stole from the rich in order to help the poor. In fact, he was a callous and brutal thief who thought nothing of attacking and killing unarmed and defenseless people.

What were "Pinkerton men"?

Allen Pinkerton (1819–1884) set up one of the first detective agencies in the United States. His employees, known as "Pinkerton men" were responsible for capturing many outlaws, including the infamous Reno Gang.

What happened to the buffalo?

Many native American tribes that lived on the great

Plains had long relied on the buffalo for their livelihoods. But once the railroads were built across the Plains, buffalo-hunting increased dramatically. Despite resistance from Native Americans, professional American buffalo-hunters came to the Plains in their thousands to shoot the seemingly limitless herds. In the south, over four million buffalo were shot between 1872 and 1874. In the north, the buffalo herd was destroyed in the early 1880s.

What were Native American reservations?

As more settlers moved into the American West, they often came into conflict with the native peoples who had been living on those lands for many generations. In the 1850s and 1860s, the American government made various treaties with the peoples of the Great Plains, establishing peaceful relations and promising them specific areas of land, known as reservations. Despite the treaties, there were many battles between the US army and Native American warriors who did not want to move on to the reservations.

What was buffalo hide used for?

In the 1870s there was a huge demand for buffalo hides. The hides were made into leather for shoes and other products. They were also used to make belts to drive the machinery in factories.

Who wanted the buffalo destroyed?

Some Americans thought that the destruction of the buffalo herds was a good thing because it would force rebellious Native American tribes into submission. Without the buffalo, they would be forced to rely on farming and government hand-outs for food. Other people were horrified and tried to stop the slaughter— but they failed.

Where did the Nez Perce go?

Whole tribes were forced to move thousands of miles to live on new reservations. The Nez Perce lived in the northwest, in Oregon. They tried to live peacefully with the settlers. But eventually violence erupted. The Nez Perces fought hard against the settlers, but they were eventually forced to move to a reservation far away in Oklahoma.

Millions of buffalo were killed by professional hunters in the early 1870s.

Who died at the Battle of Little Bighorn?

In June 1876, General George A. Custer led a group of soldiers to drive the defiant Sioux off their land in the Black Hills and on to a reservation. Custer found the Native Americans' camp at Little Bighorn on June 25, and decided to attack immediately. He did not know that at least 2,000 Native American warriors were in the camp, under their leaders Sitting Bull and Chief Crazy Horse. Custer and his men were defeated and killed by the Native Americans, sending shock waves through white American society.

The Sioux Reservation at Pine Ridge, South Dakota, in 1890.

Where did a gold rush cause problems?

In 1874, gold was discovered in the Black Hills of South Dakota. Unfortunately, the gold was on territory under the control of the Sioux and soon miners were flooding into the Black Hills, ignoring the Native Americans' rights over the land. Violence erupted, and the Sioux were ordered by the government to leave—but they refused.

What was the worst tragedy for the Sioux?

Over 150 Native Americans, including women and children, were massacred by the army at Wounded Knee, South Dakota. Twenty-five soldiers also died. After the massacre, the remaining Sioux had little choice but to move to the reservation set aside for them by the government.

Who danced the Ghost Dance?

In THE DESPERATE TIMES OF THE LATE 1800s, MANY NATIVE Americans in the West turned in hope to a new movement known as the Ghost Dance. The Ghost Dance helped Native Americans to cope with the destruction of the buffalo and the loss of their lands by promising a return to the old ways of life and better times.

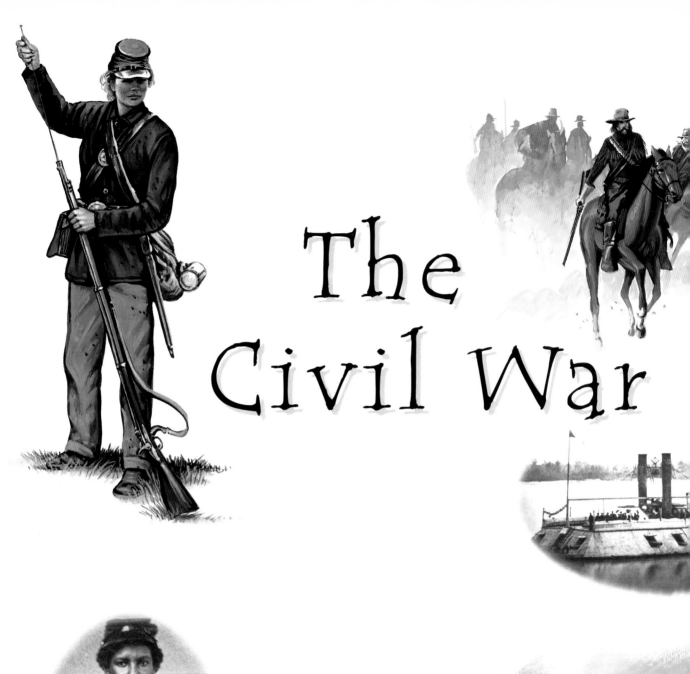

The
Civil War

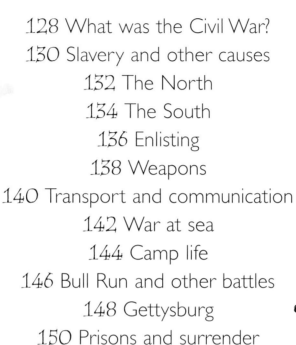

What were the two sides in the Civil War?

Confederate soldier

AMERICAN FOUGHT AGAINST AMERICAN. ON ONE SIDE were the North, or Union forces, who represented the 23 northern states of the elected government. On the other were the forces of the South, or Confederacy, who fought for the 11 Southern states. These rebel states had broken away from the Union, and elected their own president.

What did Walt Whitman say about the Civil War?

The famous poet called it that "strange, sad war." His phrase described the nature of the war perfectly. It was a war in which brother fought against brother, and a nation slaughtered its own finest men. Whitman witnessed the conflict firsthand as a volunteer in a military hospital. He also wrote: "Future years will never know the seething hell and black infernal background, and it is best they should not."

Where did the fighting take place?

The war was divided into two main areas by the Appalachian Mountains. East to the Atlantic, most battles took place in Virginia between the two capitals Washington and Richmond. To the west, the two sides fought for control of the Mississippi River. The North also blockaded the South's coast with ships in the Atlantic, and Gulf of Mexico.

Which states were in the Union?

California, Connecticut, Delaware, Illinois, Indiana, Iowa, Kansas, Kentucky, Maine, Maryland, Massachusetts, Michigan, Minnesota, Missouri, New Hampshire, New Jersey, New York, Ohio, Oregon, Pennsylvania, Rhode Island, Vermont, and Wisconsin. In addition, the "organized territories" of Colorado, Dakota, Nebraska, Nevada, New Mexico, Utah, and Washington wished to join the Union as free states.

Which states were in the Confederacy?

Alabama, Arkansas, Florida, Georgia, Louisiana, Mississippi, North and South Carolina, Tennessee, Texas, and Virginia. There were also some "border states." Rebel governments in Kentucky and Missouri supported the South.

Union soldier

Abraham Lincoln

Which was the only state ever to have two presidents?
Kentucky. The President of the Union, Abraham Lincoln, and the President of the Confederacy, Jefferson Davis, were both born in Kentucky, near the Ohio River.

How many people supported the opposing sides?
The South had a population of about 9 million people. Of these, more than 3 million were black slaves. The North found volunteers for its army in a much larger population of more than 22 million.

Which side had the most money?
The North was the center of America's big cities, industries, commerce, factories, and railroads. It boasted 75 percent of the nation's wealth. The poorer South wished to preserve its traditional world of cotton plantations worked by slaves.

What kind of war was it?
The Civil War is often described as the first "modern" war. Many modern weapons were first used in this conflict, yet the tactics were very old-fashioned. The combined result created very high casualties.

When was the Civil War?

CONFEDERATE FORCES FIRST OPENED FIRE AT FORT SUMTER, CHARLESTON, on April 12, 1861. Four years later, almost exactly, the main Confederate forces under General Robert E. Lee surrendered at Appomattox on April 9, 1865. The last Confederates surrendered on May 26.

John Brown was the leader of the abolitionists.

Who lived in *Uncle Tom's Cabin*?

A character in the novel of that name, written in 1852 by Harriet Beecher Stowe. Her sentimental story described the evils of slavery, which was an accepted practice in the Southern states. It sold 300,000 copies in its first year. The novel, and plays based on it, converted many people in the North into "abolitionists" who wished to ban slavery. It outraged many Southerners, who saw the novel as an attack on their way of life.

What was the Missouri Compromise of 1820?

In 1819, there were 11 "slave" and 11 "free" states. To preserve this balance, when the slave state of Missouri joined the Union in 1820, Maine joined as a free state. The government agreed that no new slave states north of Missouri would be admitted to the Union. For the first time, the Union had been divided into North and South.

Why do people sing about John Brown?

On October 16, 1859, fanatical abolitionist John Brown led a raid on the armory at Harper's Ferry, Virginia. He planned to steal enough weapons to lead a slave uprising in Virginia. His plan was foiled by U.S. Marines, and Brown was hanged in December. The soldiers of the North remembered Brown when they marched to war singing: "John Brown's body lies a'moldering in the grave."

Who was "Moses"?

THIS WAS THE NAME SLAVES GAVE TO HARRIET TUBMAN. AFTER ESCAPING slavery in 1849, she returned south 18 times to lead over 300 slaves to freedom. She was part of the "Underground Railroad," the secret organization that led slaves to freedom in the North.

Border ruffians wanted to force people to vote to keep slavery in Kansas.

How many black slaves were there?

There were over 3 million black slaves on the cotton plantations of the South. Slaves were recognized as property in the U.S. Constitution.

What was the Fugitive Slave Law?

A law passed as part of a new "compromise" in 1850. To keep the South happy, the law made it possible to return runaway slaves in the North to their owners. It created fury in the North. Poet Ralph Waldo Emerson called it "a filthy law."

Who smashed his cane over someone's head in the Senate?

Preston Brooks, Representative of South Carolina, beat unconscious Senator Charles Sumner, who had given a speech denouncing supporters of slavery. Brooks wrote: "The fragments of the stick are begged for as sacred relics."

Why was Abraham Lincoln elected President in 1860?

Lincoln's Republican Party, formed in 1854, was elected because the vote for the Democratic Party was split between two candidates. Lincoln became President without winning a single Southern state, many of whom refused to put his name on the poll.

Which state was the first to leave the Union?

South Carolina, which declared the Union "dissolved" on December 20, 1861. The other slave states soon followed, and on February 8 declared a new nation named the Confederate States of America.

Who were the "Border Ruffians"?

In 1854, it was decided that the inhabitants of the new territory of Kansas could vote on being a slave state or a free state. Pro-slavery gangs who rushed from Missouri to Kansas to cast illegal votes and to attack abolitionist voters were called "Border Ruffians."

Who was Abraham Lincoln?

Lincoln was president and commander-in-chief

of the North's forces. He was a striking figure, 6 ft 4 in (1.9 m) tall and a brilliant speaker. Lincoln had little military experience, but turned out to be a good commander. On March 4, 1861, he traveled to his inauguration in secret because of an assassination plot. In his speech he said: "In your hands, my dissatisfied fellow countrymen, and not in mine, is the momentous issue of civil war."

The White House was the capital of the Union.

General McClellan

Who was General Ulysses S. Grant?

Grant was the victorious commander of the North's troops at the end of the war. He had become a hero in 1862 when he demanded unconditional surrender from a Confederate general. Supporters said his initials stood for "Unconditional Surrender," and sent him so many cigars that he gave up his pipe. When prohibitionists complained that Grant drank heavily, Lincoln replied: "What brand does he drink? I'd like to send a barrel of it to the other generals."

Who were the Graybeards?

The Graybeard Regiment were all aged 45 and over. Other regiments fighting for the North were also given nicknames: Perry's Saints (all officers were ministers); La Garde Lafayette (French New Yorkers); Teacher's Regiment (mainly college professors); and Temperance Regiment (did not drink alcohol).

Who was George B. McClellan?

McClellan was commander of the North's troops in the early part of the war. His cautiousness infuriated Lincoln. When he complained about fatigued horses, Lincoln wrote: "Will you pardon me for asking what the horses of your army have done ... that could fatigue anything?"

Where was the capital of the Union?

Stars and Stripes

IT REMAINED IN WASHINGTON, WITHIN THE SLAVE STATE OF VIRGINIA. FROM the White House window, Lincoln could watch Confederate forces gathering. Until 10,000 Union troops arrived in May 1861, there was a danger that Washington would be captured.

Which songs did the North sing?

Their songs included *Yankee Doodle*, *We'll Rally Round the Flag*, and *The Girl I Left Behind Me*. *The Battle Hymn of the Republic* and *John Brown's Body* were both sung to a tune that actually came from the South.

What names were given to the Union forces?

They were known as the Union, the Federal Army, the Republic, the North, the Yanks or Yankees, and the Blues. Confederate soldiers nicknamed the Union soldiers "Billy Yank."

What flag did the North fight under?

The Stars and Stripes. War broke out when the South bombarded Fort Sumter, South Carolina, which was flying the American flag. After surrendering, the fort commander took the tattered flag away with him. He returned to rehoist the same flag four years later.

What was a black sentry supposed to have told Ulysses S. Grant?

On seeing an officer walk past smoking, the sentry is famously supposed to have said: "You must throw away that cigar, sir!"

133

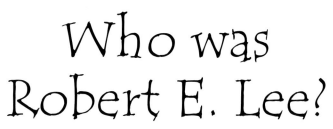

Who was Robert E. Lee?

LEE WAS THE GREATEST SOLDIER OF THE CIVIL WAR. HIS FIRST LINK TO the Civil War was when he commanded the Marines who arrested John Brown at Harper's Ferry. When the war broke out, he was offered command of the North's forces, but declined through loyalty to his home state of Virginia. He took command of the South's forces in 1862 and proved himself to be a daring and brilliant commander. His soldiers were devoted to him and named him "Marse Lee."

Who was Jefferson Davis?

Davis took the oath as President of the Confederacy on February 18, 1861. A graduate of West Point and an experienced soldier, he would have preferred a commission in the army. Just as Lee was not a supporter of slavery, so Davis was famous for his kindness to his slaves. He was imprisoned for two years after the war for treason. Seven Southern states still celebrate a legal holiday on his birthday, June 3.

How many horses were shot from under Nathan Bedford Forrest?

Forrest had 29 horses shot from under him during the war, and was frequently injured. He was a brilliant cavalry commander for the South who started the war as a private and progressed to major general. Sherman called him "the very Devil."

Was Robert E. Lee born to be a soldier?

Yes. Lee came from a famous military family. His father, Henry "Light Horse Harry" Lee, was George Washington's favorite cavalry commander. He also had ancestors who had fought with William the Conqueror and in the Crusades.

Who were the Yankee Hunters?

The Barbour County Yankee Hunters was the nickname of one of the Confederates' units. Others were the Cherokee Lincoln Killers, Hornet's Nest Riflemen, and Tallapossa Thrashers.

Robert E. Lee

Stars and Bars

Battle flag

Why did the South have two flags?

THE OFFICIAL CONFEDERATE FLAG, THE STARS AND BARS, WAS VERY SIMILAR to the Stars and Stripes. So, a red "battle flag" with stars on a blue saltire (diagonal cross) was also used. The first ones were made from silk intended for ladies' dresses.

What songs did the Confederates sing?

Their songs included *The Yellow Rose of Texas* and *The Bonnie Blue Flag*. The most famous song of the South, *Dixie*, was actually written in the North by the son of an abolitionist.

How big was the South's army?

At the start of the war, the Confederates created a regular army of 10,000 soldiers. In America, though, the tradition was for civilian volunteers to fight. In all, some one million men fought for the South.

What names were given to the Confederate forces?

They were known as the Confederates, the South, the Rebels, and the Grays. Union soldiers nicknamed their Confederate enemy "Johnny Reb."

Where was the capital of the Confederacy?

At Richmond, just 103 miles (166 km) south of Washington. When the North learned that the Confederate Congress would meet there in July 1861, the New York Tribune started a famous warcry: "Forward to Richmond! Forward to Richmond!"

The ruins of the arsenal at Richmond.

Did any women sign up to fight?

Up to 400 women disguised themselves as men so that they could enlist. They were able to do this because the doctors who examined new recruits barely looked at them. One famous soldier was Jennie Hodgers, an Irishwoman who joined the 95th Illinois Volunteers under the name of Albert Cashier. She remained undiscovered throughout the war, fighting in several major battles and receiving a pension after the armistice.

Could people avoid conscription?

Rich people on both sides could pay for a "substitute" to fight in their place. This might cost a Southern farmer up to $6,000. The arrival of unfit substitutes horrified professional soldiers. One substitute was said to have been lured from an asylum.

Did families fight on the same side?

No, the tragedy of the war was that it tore families apart. William and James Terrill were brothers who fought on opposite sides. Both rose to the rank of brigadier general and both were killed. President Lincoln's wife Mary had three half brothers who died fighting for the South.

How old were the soldiers?

ALL AGES. CURTIS KING ENLISTED IN IOWA'S "GRAYBEARDS" regiment at the ripe old age of 80. The most famous youngster in the war was Johnny Clem, the "Drummer Boy of Chickamauga." He enlisted age nine. At Chickamauga he used a sawn-off musket to shoot a Confederate officer who had shouted at him: "Surrender you little Yankee devil!" When he retired in 1915 as Major General Clem, he was the last active soldier left from the war.

A few women joined the army by pretending to be men.

136

Were all the soldiers American?

No, THEY INCLUDED ENGLISH, French, Dutch, and Hungarian soldiers, and a Scottish regiment that fought in kilts. One man listed his nationality simply as "the ocean." Native American names on the lists include Big Mush, John Bearmeat, and Warkiller Hogshooter.

Were all the soldiers white?
The Union refused to use black soldiers until 1862. After this date, nearly 180,000 black soldiers fought, and 21 were awarded the Medal of Honor. Not surprisingly, black soldiers served for the South only as servants and musicians.

Drummer boy

What did the soldiers do before the war?
The North boasted soldiers from an enormous variety of occupations, and official lists of soldiers' jobs include Paper Hanger, Gambler, Sugar Boiler, House Mover, and Loafer. Many of the South's fighters were farmers, but their lists also include Gentleman, Shoemaker, Student, Convict, and Rogue.

Did all soldiers volunteer?
No, the South passed America's first national draft law in April 1862, requiring all white males between 18 and 35 to serve for three years. In March 1863, the North conscripted all able-bodied males age between 20 and 45 (single) and 20 and 35 (married).

Who were the tallest soldiers?
David Van Buskirk, a 6 ft 11 in-(2.1 m-) soldier captured in 1862 and exhibited as the "Biggest Yankee in the World," enjoyed telling President Davis that he had six sisters taller than himself. In the Southern corner was Texan Private Henry Thruston, who measured 7 ft 7 in (2.3 m).

What famous Americans avoided the fighting?
Grover Cleveland, who later became President, hired a substitute. The famous business tycoon J.D. Rockefeller claimed to have hired 30 different substitutes.

Did all the soldiers use the same weapons?

No, VOLUNTEERS ARRIVED WITH ALL KINDS OF WEAPONS, AND BOTH governments also bought poor firearms from abroad. They were known as "pumpkin slingers" because they were so heavy and clumsy, and "mules" because they had a terrible "kick", or recoil.

How was the war similar to World War I?
As the war dragged on, regiments defended their positions by digging trenches and protecting them with wire entanglements, tripwires, earthworks, and sharpened stakes. They invented many of the tactics and defenses used in World War I.

Why did soldiers use bayonets as candlesticks?
Of all the wounds suffered in the Civil War, 94 percent were caused by bullets. Soldiers threw their bayonets away as useless, or drove them into the walls of their huts and used them as candlesticks.

Union soldiers setting up a cannon.

How did firearms develop during the Civil War?
Before the war, soldiers fired round balls from flintlock muskets with smooth barrels. These were difficult to load and usually missed their target. General Grant said the enemy could "fire at you all day without you ever finding it out." They were quickly replaced by rifles with grooves cut into the barrels, which fired pointed bullets. These were easier to load, more powerful, and deadly accurate. Both sides now had the firepower to inflict terrible casualties.

What other inventions were used in the fighting?
A primitive flame-thrower was used by one General Butler. And camouflage must have been used, as Confederate troops wrote about shooting down "moving bushes."

Who threw watermelons?

The Dictator was the name given to a giant 17,000-pound mortar, as tall as a man, which lobbed iron cannonballs the size of watermelons on to the enemy lines. Artillerymen chalked their names and addresses on these missiles before firing them.

Was germ warfare ever used?

No, but it was suggested. A Louisiana slave owner named R. Barrow wrote to Congress with a plan to send the corpse of a man who had died from yellow fever into New Orleans to start an epidemic there.

Who invented the land mine?

GENERAL GABRIEL RAINS OF NORTH CAROLINA DEVELOPED LAND mines for the South, which he called "land torpedoes." They were set off by pressure or tripwires. General Sherman forced Confederate soldiers to dig up these "infernal machines."

Who first used a machine gun?

In 1862. The North first used their "Union repeating gun" in a skirmish near Harper's Ferry. It was known as a "coffee mill gun" because it was operated by turning a crank, which operated a revolving cylinder. The Confederates invented their own machine gun, called the Williams gun, and claimed to have first inflicted casualties with it at Seven Pines in May 1862.

Confederate soldiers with a battery of cannons.

New York Herald correspondents sketched and wrote notes on what they saw on the battlefield.

Correspondents sit outside the New Yo[rk] Herald wagon.

What brought the war to the people back home?

For the first time, photographers stumbled on to battlegrounds with their heavy equipment and asked soldiers to remain still while their photos were taken. The most famous photographer was New York's Mathew B. Brady. He shocked New York City in 1862 with an exhibition of photos of the dead. One visitor noted: "If he has not brought bodies and laid them in our dooryards, he has done something very like it."

Who blew up bridges?

IN REVENGE FOR THE MANY ATTACKS ON HIS TRANSPORT SYSTEM, HAUPT wrote an instruction manual showing Union troops how to destroy Confederate railroads. He also invented the tools for the job: a rail-bending "hook" and a "torpedo" for blowing up bridges.

Who had the best horses?

At the beginning of the war, troops from the rural South were much the better cavalry. They were allowed to ride their own thoroughbreds, and came from a tradition of excellent cavalrymen.

Who invented a horseshoe machine?

The Union had much better technology. They invented a horseshoe machine that could produce 60 horseshoes a minute. As the South's mounts and equipment became exhausted, the North's improved.

Who traveled by rail?

The North, which had a more advanced rail system, was able to transport its troops, heavy guns, and supplies from east to west much more quickly than the South. For many soldiers, the journey to the front was their first experience of a train journey.

What went up in the air to spy on the enemy?

Hot air balloons were used to spy on enemy positions. They were pioneered by showman Thaddeus Lowe, who founded the U.S. Balloon Corps after demonstrating a balloon to the president. From 300 ft (92 m), the pilot could help his gunners to aim, or relay details of enemy troop positions by telegraph. One balloon flew from the barge *George Washington Parke Custis*—making the barge the world's first aircraft carrier.

Who used telescopes, flashlights, and telegraph?

Albert J. Myer founded the U.S. Army Signal Corps. He trained units of men to use telescopes, flags, flashlights and the recent invention of the telegraph to set up a communications network for the North. By the end of the war, the vast army was linked with thousands of miles of telegraph wire.

Who built rubber boats for spies?

Brigadier General Herman Haupt was the North's transportation chief. His engineering genius masterminded the Union's excellent railroad system. He also built fortified and portable bridges, and portable rubber boats for spies. When Confederates sabotaged the North's railroads, Haupt's Construction Corps repaired them with incredible speed.

Who were the spies?

Spies operated on both sides. The Union had a famous secret agent named Timothy Webster, who was hanged in 1862 for spying. The Confederates had a famous woman spy called Belle Boyd, who was known as the Siren of the Shenandoah.

Who was Allan Pinkerton?

Pinkerton had famously set up one of the first private detective agencies in 1850. After the war started, he escorted Lincoln to his inauguration and started a "secret service" for the Union.

The railroad was very new to the United States during the Civil War.

The *St. Louis* was the first ironclad gunboat built in the United States.

What were "ironclads"?

THE "IRONCLADS" WERE A NEW TYPE OF SHIP THAT LOOKED MORE LIKE submarines. They had steam-driven propellers and were covered in armor plating. The first was the South's *Merrimac*, an old frigate covered with flattened railroad tracks. She sunk three of the North's ships on March 8, 1862. The following day she battled with the North's own ironclad *Monitor* in the first sea battle between these strange craft. This is the point in history where traditional wooden warships began to be replaced by modern battleships.

When did a submarine first sink a ship?
On February 17, 1864, the Confederate submarine *Hunley* attacked the Union ship *Housatonic*. The submarine was powered by eight infantrymen operating hand cranks. Her designer Horace L. Hunley had been killed during trial runs of this dangerous device, along with several crew members. The *Hunley* attacked with a "torpedo," which was actually a mine attached to a spear on the submarine's nose. The explosion sunk the ship—but also the submarine.

Who would not surrender?
Under the command of Captain James Iredell Waddell, the Confederate ship *Shenandoah* roamed the Atlantic Ocean sinking Union shipping. Waddell ignored messages saying the war was over and continued fighting. He did not surrender until seven months after the South's surrender.

What snake set out to strangle the South?

"Scott's Anaconda" was the nickname given to the North's naval blockade of the South. It was designed to work like a great snake, strangling the South by cutting off their supplies, and was suggested by General Winfield Scott.

How did Britain pay for the war?

The Geneva Tribunal of Arbitration decided in 1872 that Britain had not remained neutral because it helped built Confederate ships. She had to pay the United States $15.5 million for damages these ships did to the Union navy.

Was the Civil War fought only on land?

No, Union ships blockaded the South and supported their armies from the Mississippi. Confederate raiders fought back by attacking the North's merchant shipping. The North's powerful navy grew to 670 ships, and the South's to 130.

How did the Mississippi River help the North?

By controlling the Mississippi, the North divided the South into two and was able to contain the fighting within a certain area. It could also support and supply its troops by running ships up and down the river.

Who flushed a toilet underwater?

The eccentric but brilliant Swedish engineer John Ericsson designed the first ironclads used by the North. He also invented the screw propeller, revolving gun turrets, an anchor with four flukes (the arrows that stick in the sea-bed), and a flush toilet that worked below the waterline.

Who painted the Civil War in the English Channel?

The great French painter Manet depicted the sinking of the famous Confederate raider *Alabama* by the North's *Kearsage* in the English Channel. Under the command of the brilliant Captain Raphael Semmes, the *Alabama* had gained her fame by defeating 65 Union ships.

Who fired the first torpedo?

IN OCTOBER 1862, THE SOUTH CREATED THE TORPEDO SERVICE. IT WAS responsible for laying the mines—then called "torpedoes" —in harbors and rivers, which sank 43 Union ships. The most common "Rains" torpedoes (named after their inventor) were made from beer kegs.

Submarines were very dangerous and unsophisticated vessels. Many men were killed in them.

A makeshift church houses a Catholic service.

What uniforms did the soldiers wear?

Officially, the South wore gray and the North wore blue. But this was a war of amateur soldiers, who reported for duty in uniforms ranging from kilts to busbies. One Southern captain fought in jaguar-skin trousers with matching holsters!

Did the soldiers have time to go to church?
The church tried to support the soldiers and prevent them from spending too much time gambling and drinking. There were regular services.

Which regiment hoped to put their feet up?
The Union's 7th New York Unit, which contained fashion-conscious soldiers from Grammarcy Park, marched off to war with 1,000 velvet-covered footstools.

How were soldiers punished for misbehaving?
When they became bored during lulls in the fighting, soldiers regularly fought, gambled, thieved, and got drunk on whiskies with names like "Bust Skull." Soldiers also deserted, sometimes so that they could receive money for re-enlisting. Punishments were designed to humiliate: having your head shaved, wearing a sign showing your crime, being paraded in a barrel or being sat on an enormous wooden horse. Flogging was illegal, but branding (with a hot iron) was common.

Camp life could be very boring, so soldiers played a lot of card games that often involved gambling.

What were soldiers supposed to eat?

Both sides had generous rations at the beginning of the war. The official daily issue for each soldier was 12 oz (300 g) of pork or 1 lb 4 oz (600 g) of beef; 1 lb (500 g) of hardtack or 1 lb 4 oz (600 g) of corn; plus beans, rice, coffee, sugar, salt, and pepper.

Which regiment had the most famous mascot?

The 8th Wisconsin Regiment had an eagle named Old Abe as their mascot. Three of the bearers, who carried Old Abe into battle on a perch, were shot from under him, but he lived to enjoy great fame until 1881.

The mess kitchen was a makeshift wooden building.

What were "worm castles"?

THE BISCUITS CALLED "HARDTACK," WHICH WERE THE SOLDIERS' STAPLE DIET.

Soldiers called them "worm castles" because they became infested with maggots and weevils in storage. They were also known as "teeth-dullers" and "sheet-iron crackers" because they were so hard you had to soak them in coffee or break them with a rifle butt. Hardtack was so maggoty that one soldier said: "All the fresh meat we had came in the hard bread."

How could a gun grind coffee?

A few lucky soldiers had coffee-mills built into their rifles. This showed how much coffee was valued. When the Union blockade caused shortages, Rebel soldiers had to drink substitutes made from peanuts and potatoes.

Did the soldiers have enough to eat?

Both sides produced enough to feed their troops, but the South did not have the railroads to transport supplies properly or the salt to preserve it. Starvation at the end of the war caused some Confederate troops to mutiny.

What was "salt horse"?

This was the soldiers' name for the beef they were given, which was pickled with enough salt for it to last two years. One soldier complained that the meat was so bad the buzzards would not eat it.

Fort Sumter

What was the first big battle?

THE FIRST MAJOR ENGAGEMENT OF THE WAR TOOK PLACE ON JULY 21, 1861,

at Bull Run. The glory of war that some troops had imagined became a horrific reality. A Union officer said of his troops: "They seemed to be paralyzed, standing with their eyes and mouths wide open, and did not seem to hear me." The Union suffered a surprise defeat, and realized that a quick victory would not be theirs.

What happened at Fort Sumter?

Confederate artillery started bombarding the Union's Fort Sumter, near Charleston Harbor on April 12, 1861. The following day, the fort commander surrendered. More importantly, the attack had signaled the start of the war.

What was the bloodiest day of the war?

The forces of General Lee and General McClellan met at Antietam Creek, near the town of Sharpsburg. In the single bloodiest day of the war, 10,000 Confederate and 12,000 Union soldiers were killed or wounded.

Who panicked at Bull Run?

Amazingly, the battle was watched by sightseers, including some congressmen, who had traveled down in buggies from Washington. Dressed in their fine clothes, they set up their picnics near the battlefield so they could watch the 75,000 troops do battle. When the Union forces started their retreat, these panicking spectators helped turn it into a rout that almost reached Washington.

Generals and commanders often viewed the battles from a safe distance.

How did Thomas J. Jackson become known as "Stonewall"?

General Jackson became Lee's right-hand man in the war. At Bull Run, a Confederate general rallied his troops by pointing at Jackson and crying: "There stands Jackson like a stone wall! Rally behind the Virginians!"

What did it mean to "see the elephant"?

It was the troops' nickname for fighting the enemy for the first time. It must have been a terrifying experience. The phrase was taken from farm boys, who expressed wonder at "seeing the elephant" after visiting the circus for the first time.

Who was Elmer E. Ellsworth?

The famous 24-year-old colonel was the first officer to die in the war. He led the first Union troops to go South. When he was shot by an innkeeper while taking down a Confederate flag in Alexandria, the North was outraged.

What famous battles were fought in the first part of the war?

Important battles and campaigns included Bull Run (July 16, 1861), the Shenandoah Valley Campaign (December 1861 to June 1862), the Seven Days' Battles (June 25 to July 1, 1862), Antietam Creek (September 17, 1862), Fredericksburg (December 13, 1862), and Chancellorsville (May 2, 1862).

"Stonewall" Jackson was seen as a brave leader of men.

Who killed "Stonewall" Jackson?

At the battle of Chancellorsville, Jackson was mistakenly shot by his own troops. He had an arm amputated and died—like many soldiers—from illness caused by his wounds.

What did Confederate troops hope to capture at Honey Springs?

Slaves. The Confederates took slave shackles with them into battle at Honey Springs on July 17th, 1863, because they were fighting against black Union troops whom they expected to capture. In fact, this battle in Indian Territory was won by the 1st Kansas Colored Volunteers.

The Gettysburg address is still known as one of the greatest speeches of all time.

What is the Gettysburg Address?

So many men died at Gettysburg that a cemetery covering 17 acres was created there. When Lincoln dedicated it on November 19, 1863, he made the Gettysburg Address—one of the most famous speeches in American history.

What was Pickett's charge?

12,000 infantrymen slowly advanced in a straight line under General George Pickett right into the mouths of the Union artillery. As they marched forward, the Union artillery cut them down in their thousands. It made a noise "strange and terrible, a sound that came from thousands of human throats ... like a vast mournful roar." When Pickett was asked to reorganize his division, he replied: "General Lee, I have no division now."

Three Confederate soldiers, captured during the battle of Gettysburg.

What was the Battle of Gettysburg?

THE MOST FAMOUS BATTLE EVER FOUGHT ON AMERICAN SOIL. AN ARMY OF 75,000 Confederate soldiers attacked 87,000 entrenched Union troops at the market town of Gettysburg, Pennsylvania, from July 1 to 3, 1863. When the South's charge on the final day was cut down, any hope for a Confederate victory in the war was lost.

Why did the men of Pickett's charge stop advancing?

Even as the cannonballs flew among them, they stopped to make sure that their line was straight. One of the Union soldiers mumbled in horrified disbelief: "My God! They're dressing the line."

Who were the commanding officers at Gettysburg?

The Union forces were commanded by General George Meade. During the battle he was said to be "quick, bold, cheerful, and hopeful." The Confederates were commanded by Robert E. Lee, who repeated sadly after Pickett's charge: "It's all my fault."

How many soldiers died at Gettysburg?

Lee lost 28,000 men, while Meade lost 23,000. Some regiments were virtually wiped out. The 26th North Carolina Infantry lost 708 dead and wounded out of 800 men.

Who died without firing a shot?

SOME OF THE SOLDIERS AT GETTYSBURG WERE COMPLETELY UNTRAINED

and had never even fired a rifle in action. After the battle, many single-shot rifles were found stuffed with up to 10 charges. Their owners had kept reloading them without ever managing to fire them.

Who put his own bones in a museum?

Major General Daniel Sickles was a Union general who was struck by a cannonball at Gettysburg. His leg had to be amputated, and he instructed the bones to be sent to the Army Medical Museum, where he visited them for many years.

What famous battles were fought in the later part of the war?

Famous engagements and campaigns included the capture of Vicksburg (July 1, 1863), Chickamagua (September 19—20, 1863), the Battle of the Wilderness (May 5—6, 1864), and the Siege of Petersburg (June 1864—April 1865).

General Lee was a brilliant leader and battle tactician.

What happened to captured soldiers?

Many captured soldiers on both sides were kept in terrible prison camps. Andersonville Prison in Georgia was the worst of these. More than one in three of the Union soldiers held there died from starvation and disease, a total of some 13,000 men. Photographs taken of prisoners, who somehow survived show the terrible effects, of starvation. Former inmates of one prison weighed less than 100 lb (45 kg).

Who was Henry Wirz?

Captain Henry Wirz was the Swiss commander of the prison at Andersonville. The press named him the "Andersonville Savage," and after a show trial he was found guilty of war crimes and hanged in front of a huge crowd.

How many soldiers died in prison?

About 194,000 Union soldiers were held prisoner, and 30,000 of them died. Some 214,000 Confederate soldiers were held in prison camps in the North, where 26,000 died.

Where did General Lee surrender?

AT 3:00 P.M. ON PALM SUNDAY, APRIL 9, 1865, LEE SIGNED the surrender at the courthouse in Appomattox, Virginia. Under the terms agreed with General Grant, all Confederate soldiers could return home without facing trial for treason. Lee also made a special request that those cavalrymen with their own horses might be allowed to take them back to their homes.

What is Providence Spring?

At ANDERSONVILLE, THE DRINKING WATER WAS FILTHY. BUT IN August 1864, after a rainstorm, a spring of pure, clean water bubbled up from the ground. The prisoners, believing it was a sign that God had not forgotten them, called it Providence Spring. It still flows today.

What vandal led the "March to the Sea"?

At the end of 1864, the North's Major General William Tecumseh Sherman led his troops through Georgia from Atlanta to the coast. The "Vandal Chief" used a new form of warfare, burning or seizing property to break the will of the civilian population.

How many battles were there?

The war lasted for 1,489 days, from the capture of Fort Sumter on April 12, 1861, until the last battle at Palmito Ranch on May 12, 1865 (Lee was not the last to surrender). In this time there were over 10,000 engagements, big and small, between the two sides.

What happened to the armies after the Confederates surrendered?

After turning in their arms, Confederate soldiers were simply left to make their own way home. The roads were soon crowded with them. Ships and trains carried the Union troops to their home states, where they were paid and discharged.

What horror happened on board *The Sultana*?

The Sultana was a paddle steamer designed to carry 370 passengers. On April 24, 1865, she left Vicksburg with 2,000 freed Union prisoners aboard. When her boiler exploded, 1,700 men who had survived the horrors of prisoner-of-war camps perished in the inferno.

Confederate soldiers return home.

Clara Barton helped many
wounded soldiers.

What operation was most often performed on the battlefield?

Three out of four operations performed in the field hospitals were amputations. The bullets fired by civil war rifles inflicted terrible damage. Surgeons regarded amputation as the only way to stop disease spreading in badly injured limbs. But their equipment was never sterilized, and it was quite rare for a surgeon to wash his hands or instruments between operations.

Why were casualties so high?

The poor soldiers in the civil war were fighting a battle at the worst point in history. Advances in weapons meant that the ability to kill and wound had suddenly increased. But the surgeon's ability to mend and heal had not yet entered the modern age.

How did smugglers get quinine and morphine to their troops?

Women and children sometimes carried dolls from the North to the South. In the hollow heads and bodies were precious medical supplies.

Who was Clara Barton?

SHE WAS A NEW ENGLAND WOMAN WHO WORKED IN A PATENT

office. She placed an advert in a newspaper asking for medical supplies, then carried them to the battlefield. There she provided a soup kitchen and offered bandages and medicine to the wounded. After the war, in 1881, she founded the American Red Cross. A senator said: "She has the talent of a statesman, the command of a general, and the heart and hand of a woman."

Hospitals were often makeshift and unhygienic.

Which side had the best medical services?

All the major pharmacies were located in the North. Two government laboratories were set up in 1863, employing chemists and 350 workers to make medicines and pills.

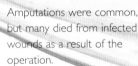

Amputations were common, but many died from infected wounds as a result of the operation.

How many soldiers died in the Civil War?

IN THE CIVIL WAR, 620,000 MEN LOST THEIR LIVES, WHICH IS MORE than in all the United State's other wars combined. Of these, 60 percent died from disease. As a comparison, in World War II, 405,000 American troops lost their lives.

What were hospital standards like in 1861?

Doctors had no antibiotics, no understanding of bacteria or sterilization, and no knowledge of the connection between filthy water and disease. If they survived their wounds, patients were likely to die from typhoid, dysentery, or pneumonia.

What did Louisa May Alcott say about hospitals?

The famous author of *Little Women*, who worked as a Union nurse in the war, wrote: "A more perfect pestilence box than this I never saw—cold, damp, dirty, full of vile odors from wounds, kitchens, and stables."

What drugs were successful?

To treat malaria, doctors had quinine, which is still used for that purpose today. Opium was an effective painkiller, but soldiers became addicted to it. Chloroform was used as an anaesthetic.

Lincoln was shot in this box at Ford's theater.

What did John Wilkes Booth do at the theater?

On the evening of Good Friday, April 14, 1865, the actor rushed into Lincoln's box at Ford's Theater and fired a single pistol shot into the president's head. He then leapt from the box, breaking his leg but still managing to escape. Lincoln died the following morning. Booth was later killed. Strangely, Booth had been present at the hanging of John Brown just before the war began.

Why did Lincoln not want to go to the theater?

He had had a clear dream in which he foresaw his own death. In this dream, which he recounted to his wife, he saw himself lying in his coffin.

When did the Civil War end slavery?

OFFICIALLY, ACCORDING TO THE EMANCIPATION Proclamation that Lincoln had made during the war, it ended on January 1, 1863. Actually, votes for blacks were first put into force in the South in 1867.

Payne, one of Booth's associates was arrested for the murder of Lincoln.

What happened to Robert E. Lee?

HE BECAME PRESIDENT OF WASHINGTON COLLEGE

in Lexington, Virginia. After his defeat, he said: "I believe it to be the duty of everyone to unite in the restoration of the country, and the establishment of peace and harmony."

What were "carpetbaggers"?

This was the name given to Northerners who traveled to the South to try to influence how the defeated states were run. The term suggested that they turned up in the South with only enough possessions to fill the cheap suitcase known as a carpetbag. Some carpetbaggers went South to make money, some for high political office, some to ensure the black population used the power to vote that they had been given.

What did Walt Whitman write about Lincoln's funeral?

He wrote the famous poem *When lilacs last in the dooryard bloom'd*, which ended: "With the tolling tolling bells' perpetual clang, Here, coffin that slowly passes, I give you my sprig of lilac."

What was Jefferson Davis wearing when he was captured?

When he was captured by Union cavalry on May 10, 1865, he was emerging from a tent wearing a shawl given to him by his wife. This led to stories in the North that he had been trying to escape dressed in skirts and a bonnet.

What was the Ku Klux Klan?

After the war, some Southerners tried to scare blacks away from the polling booths by forming this secret society, whose members wore masked uniforms, named shrouds, and burned crosses. Among the new members was cavalry hero Nathan Bedford Forrest.

How did the Civil War affect baseball?

Union soldiers from New York City played the game wherever they went. The rules gradually spread around the battlegrounds, and after the war it began to gain great popularity.

Union soldiers play baseball during the Civil War.

Presidents

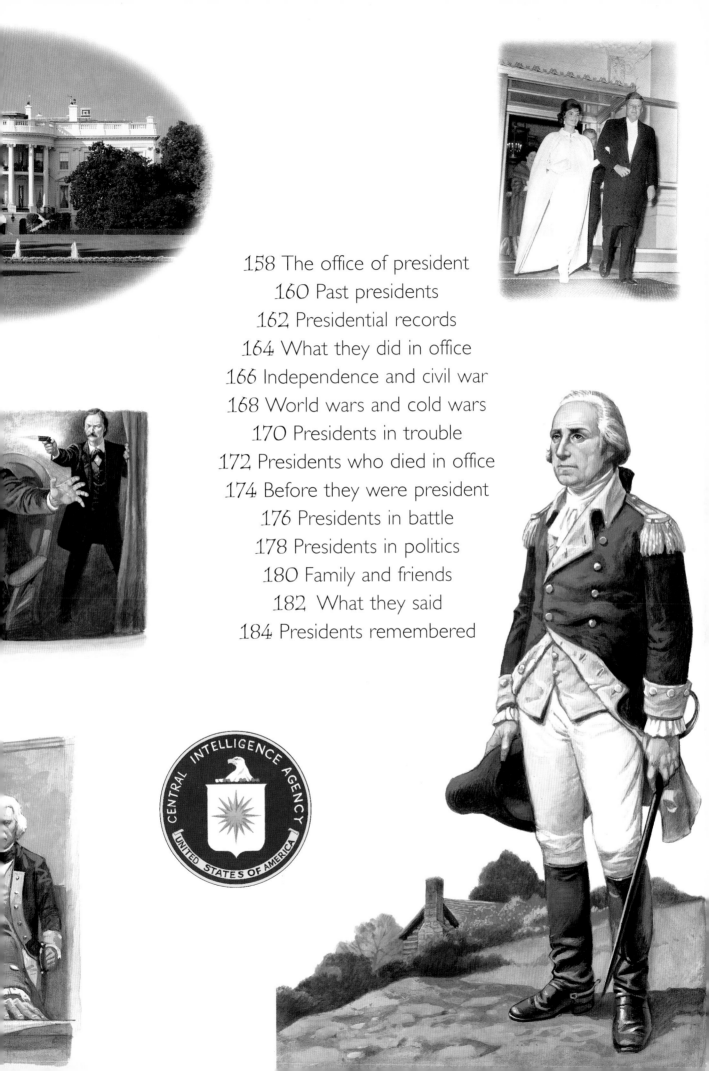

CENTRAL INTELLIGENCE AGENCY
UNITED STATES OF AMERICA

What is the president's job?
The president is in charge of the United States of America. His list of jobs includes being head of the government administration and foreign policy. He chooses people to head government departments (the Secretaries of State, the Treasury, Defense, and so on), and he is Commander-in-Chief of the U.S. Army and U.S. Navy.

What is the Oval Office?
The Oval Office is the President's private office in the West Wing of the White House. It was added to the White House in 1909.

Who can be president?
You have to be at least 35 years old, a natural citizen of the U.S., and you must have lived in the U.S. for at least 14 years. Of course, you have to be elected too!

Where does the president live?

THE PRESIDENT'S OFFICIAL HOME ADDRESS IS 1600 PENNSYLVANIA AVENUE, Washington, D.C., commonly known as the White House. As well as private rooms for the president and his family, the White House also has dozens of public function rooms and government offices. All of the presidents have lived at the White House, since 1800 when the second president, John Adams, and his wife Abigail, moved in.

What is a presidential term?
The time that a president stays in office. A term always begins at noon on January 20, when one president steps down and the new president is inaugurated. The term ends exactly four years later.

The White House was burnt down during the British invasion in 1814 but rebuilt in the 1820s.

Who chooses the president?

The people of the U.S.! In the November of the year before a presidential term ends, the people in each state vote for people called electors. The electors then vote for the presidential candidates from each political party. The candidate who gains the majority of votes wins.

How long can a person be president?

The maximum time that a president can serve for is two complete terms, or eight years. Then he must step down. The rule was introduced in 1951.

What does the vice-president do?

The vice-president is elected along with the president as his "running mate"—a sort of second-in-command. The vice-president acts as president of the Senate, and takes over as president for the rest of the term if the president dies.

The president's airplane has to be very secure as well as having the latest technology to keep the president in touch with his staff.

Who is the first lady?

The first lady is the president's wife. Traditionally, she organizes functions and acts as hostess at the White House. She also becomes involved in social issues and charities.

Will there ever be a first man?

There's no reason why not, since there's nothing to prevent a woman from becoming president.

What is Air Force One?

THE AIRPLANE THAT THE PRESIDENT AND THE WHITE HOUSE STAFF USE WHEN THEY travel on official business. Air Force One is operated by the U.S. Air Force, and is currently a Boeing 747.

Who was the first president?

GEORGE WASHINGTON WAS ELECTED FIRST PRESIDENT IN 1789. WASHINGTON led the Continental army against the British during the American Revolution, after which the United States was formed and became an independent country. Washington was president for two terms in office. He died in 1799.

Washington declined a third term as president.

Which presidents were also vice-presidents?

Adams, Jefferson, Van Buren, Nixon, Ford, and Bush, who were later elected president, and Tyler, Fillmore, Andrew Johnson, Arthur, Theodore Roosevelt, Coolidge, Truman, and Lyndon Johnson, who took over on the death of the president.

Which president was never elected?

Gerald Ford. He became vice-president in 1973 when Vice-president Agnew resigned. He became President Ford in 1974 when President Nixon himself resigned.

Which president lost but won?

In the 1888 election, only 48% of the people voted for Benjamin Harrison versus 49% for his opponent Grover Cleveland. But more electors voted for Harrison, and he won by 233 to 168.

How many presidents have there been?

Up to and including Bill Clinton, there have been 42 presidents of the U.S. They are ...

1	1789	George Washington (1732—1799)
2	1797	John Adams (1735—1826)
3	1801	Thomas Jefferson (1743—1826)
4	1809	James Madison (1751—1836)
5	1817	James Monroe (1758—1831)
6	1825	John Quincy Adams (1767—1848)
7	1829	Andrew Jackson (1767—1845)
8	1837	Martin Van Buren (1782—1862)
9	1841	William Henry Harrison (1773—1841)
10	1841	John Tyler (1790—1841)
11	1845	James Knox Polk (1795—1849)
12	1849	Zachary Taylor (1784—1849)
13	1850	Millard Fillmore (1800—1874)
14	1853	Franklin Pierce (1804—1869)
15	1857	James Buchanan (1791—1868)
16	1861	Abraham Lincoln (1809—1865)
17	1865	Andrew Johnson (1808—1875)
18	1869	Ulysses Simpson Grant (1822—1885)
19	1877	Rutherford Birchard Hayes (1822—1893)
20	1881	James Abram Garfield (1831—1881)
21	1881	Chester Alan Arthur (1830—1886)
22	1885	Grover Cleveland (1837—1908)
23	1889	Benjamin Harrison (1833—1901)
24	1893	Grover Cleveland (1837—1908)
25	1897	William McKinley (1843—1901)
26	1901	Theodore Roosevelt (1858—1919)
27	1909	William Howard Taft (1857—1930)
28	1913	Woodrow Wilson (1856—1924)
29	1921	Warren Gamaliel Harding (1865—1923)
30	1923	Calvin Coolidge (1872—1933)
31	1929	Herbert Clark Hoover (1874—1964)
32	1933	Franklin Delano Roosevelt (1882—1945)
33	1945	Harry S Truman (1884—1972)
34	1953	Dwight David Eisenhower (1890—1969)
35	1961	John Fitzgerald Kennedy (1917—1963)
36	1963	Lyndon Baines Johnson (1908—1973)
37	1969	Richard Milhous Nixon (1913—1994)
38	1974	Gerald Rudolph Ford (1913—)
39	1977	James Earl Carter (1924—)
40	1981	Ronald Wilson Reagan (1911—)
41	1989	George Herbert Walker Bush (1924—)
42	1993	William Jefferson Clinton (1946—)

Under Van Buren, the U.S. went to war with the Seminole Indians.

Who was the first all-American president?

MARTIN VAN BUREN WAS THE FIRST PRESIDENT born as an American citizen. The presidents before him were born before the Declaration of Independence in 1776, and so were officially British citizens.

Theodore Roosevelt won the Nobel Peace Prize in 1905 for trying to help resolve the Russo-Japanese war.

Who was the youngest president?

THEODORE ROOSEVELT, THE 26TH PRESIDENT. HE WAS ELECTED vice-president in the 1900 elections and became president in September 1901 after the assassination of President McKinley. He was just 42 years old at the time. He was easily reelected for a second term in 1904.

Who was president most briefly?

The 9th president, William Henry Harrison. He was in office from March 4 to April 4, 1841. Harrison was 68 years old when he was inaugurated, and died from pneumonia exactly one month later.

Who was reelected the most times?

Franklin Delano Roosevelt was the only president to be elected three times (1932, 1936, and 1940), and he was elected again (1944) to make a record four times.

Who was the oldest president?

Ronald Reagan, who was 69 years old when he was inaugurated in January 1981. Reagan was reelected in 1984, and was 77 when he left office in 1989.

Who was elected again after defeat?
President Grover Cleveland is the only president to have served two terms separated by another presidency (that of Benjamin Harrison).

Who was the youngest elected president?
John F. Kennedy was elected as president in 1961 at the age of 44. He narrowly defeated Richard Nixon in the election.

Which presidents resigned?
Only President Richard Nixon, on August 9, 1974, halfway through his second term. He resigned because of the Watergate affair.

Which state have most presidents come from?
Virginia, where eight presidents have been born, including four of the first five. Next comes Ohio, with seven. President Clinton was the first president from Arkansas.

Franklin D. Roosevelt lost the use of his legs as a result of the illness, polio, in 1921.

Who was president longest?

FRANKLIN DELANO ROOSEVELT, WHO HELD OFFICE FOR MORE than 12 years. He was elected in 1932 and again in 1936. In 1940 he became the first and only president to be elected for a third term. In 1944 he was elected again, but died suddenly in office in 1945. This was before the presidency was restricted to two terms.

The CIA was linked with the Watergate scandal and was criticized by many people.

Who started the CIA?

THE CIA (CENTRAL INTELLIGENCE AGENCY) WAS FORMED DURING THE administration of President Harry S. Truman in 1947. Its job is to collect and interpret information about other countries. In the past it has been accused of interfering in the internal affairs of countries, including the U.S..

Who signed salt for peace?
SALT is short for Strategic Arms Limitation Talks. These were negotiations between the United States and the former Soviet Union to stop production of nuclear missiles. SALT I (1972) was signed by President Nixon and Soviet leader Leonid Brezhnev. SALT II (1979) was signed by Leonid Brezhnev and President Carter.

Who made the U.S. twice as big?

In 1803, PRESIDENT JEFFERSON AGREED TO BUY AN AREA OF LAND KNOWN AS the Louisiana Territory from France. It stretched from the Mississippi River to the Rocky Mountains, and cost just $15 million.

Jefferson was a very good scholar and was the main writer of the Declaration of Independence.

Which president helped abolish slavery?

Abraham Lincoln. Slavery was the main reason for the Civil War (1861—1865), between the northern states (the Unionists), which wanted slavery abolished, and the southern states (the Confederates), which wanted to keep it. Lincoln was president of the victorious Union during the war.

Who invented the cabinet?

The cabinet is a committee made up of the heads of the government departments. It was George Washington's idea. Originally it had just four members—the secretaries of State, the Treasury, War, and the Attorney General.

Who was the Great Conservationist?

Theodore Roosevelt, the 26th president. He warned people about the dangers of using up the world's natural resources, and established the first wildlife refuge at Pelican Island, Florida.

Who had a hotline to Russia?

In the early 1960s, President Kennedy called for an end to the Cold War between the West, led by the United States, and the East, led by the former Soviet Union (often called Russia). A special telephone line was connected between the White House and the Kremlin, the residence of the Soviet leader, so that the leaders could talk in times of crisis.

Who lost the White House in 1812?

The War of 1812 (which lasted from 1812 to 1815) was fought between the United States and Britain. In 1814, President James Madison fled from the White House before it was captured and burned out by the British.

Who reinforced the East Coast?

In 1823, President James Monroe announced that the United States would not put up with any more European interference in America. He supervised construction of a chain of defenses on the East Coast of the United States to resist invasions.

Which president led a revolution?

BEFORE BECOMING THE FIRST PRESIDENT OF THE UNITED STATES,

George Washington was an army officer. In the War of Independence against the British, General Washington led the Continental army, which he turned from a band of farmers into a fighting force. After five years of fighting, the turning point of the war came in 1781, when the main British force surrendered at Yorktown.

Washington was a distinguished soldier who co-ordinated his generals well against the British.

Andrew Jackson became a hero after defeating the British at New Orleans.

Who won a war with Mexico?

James Knox Polk. He was president during the Mexican War (1846—1848), and fought over the position of the border between Mexico and the United States. The United States won half of Mexico.

When were there two presidents?

During the Civil War (1861—1865), 11 states left the United States (the Union) to form the Union of Confederate States (the Confederacy). Abraham Lincoln was president of the Union, and Jefferson Davis was president of the Confederacy.

Which hero was called hickory?

ANDREW "OLD HICKORY" JACKSON. AS MAJOR General Jackson, he led a force of volunteers to victory against the Creek Indians in 1814, and also defeated the British in the Battle of New Orleans in 1815.

Who lost seven states?

James Buchanan, who was president before Abraham Lincoln. Near the end of his presidency, the states of Alabama, Florida, Georgia, Louisiana, Mississippi, South Carolina, and Texas left the Union before the start of the Civil War.

... and who got them back?

Abraham Lincoln, president of the victorious Union side during the Civil War (1861—1865). He was assassinated a few days after the war ended.

Who declared war on Spain?

The 25th president, William McKinley. He declared war on Spain in 1898 because the Spanish would not leave Cuba. The United States won the war after defeating Spain in sea and land battles.

In the attack on Pearl Harbor, 2,400 people were killed, and 300 aircraft and 18 ships were destroyed.

Who declared war in 1917?
President Woodrow Wilson ordered U.S. ships to be armed against attacks by German submarines in March 1917. War was declared the following month.

Who dropped the nuclear bomb on Japan?
Harry S. Truman took over as president in 1945, when World War II was still being fought. Truman authorized two nuclear bombs to be dropped on Japanese cities to force the Japanese to surrender quickly.

Who led the U.S. into World War II?

JAPAN ATTACKED THE U.S. NAVAL BASE AT PEARL HARBOR, HAWAII, IN 1941.
Franklin D. Roosevelt was president at the time. The United States immediately declared war. Roosevelt was president and Commander-in-Chief of the U.S. armed forces until he died shortly before the end of war.

What was the Bay of Pigs?

In 1961, President Kennedy approved a plan for the CIA to help Cuban refugees invade Cuba and overthrow communist leader Fidel Castro. The invasion failed at the Bay of Pigs on Cuba's southern coast.

Who ended the crisis in Cuba?

In 1963, there were rumors that the Soviet Union was putting nuclear missiles on Cuba. The Soviets withdrew when President Kennedy promised that the U.S. would not invade Cuba.

Who stayed away from the Olympics?

After the Soviet Union invaded Afghanistan in 1979, President Carter protested by ordering a boycott of the 1980 Moscow Olympics. Sixty-three other nations joined the boycott and refused to attend.

Who made war in the Gulf?

After Iraqi forces invaded Kuwait in 1990, President Bush announced operation Desert Shield to protect neighboring countries in the Persian Gulf. In 1991, U.S. troops led operation Desert Storm to recapture Kuwait.

Who sent troops to Vietnam?

IN THE MID 1960S, PRESIDENT JOHNSON SENT NEARLY HALF A MILLION TROOPS TO South Vietnam to fight against communist attacks from North Vietnam. The troops were withdrawn by President Nixon in the early 1970s.

Who shot down a U-2?

During the Cold War, a U-2 spy plane of the U.S. Air Force was shot down over the Soviet Union with its pilot Francis Gary Powers. President Eisenhower defended the flight, saying that it was necessary for national security.

Who became president in a plane?

Lyndon B. Johnson took over as president when President Kennedy was assassinated in Dallas in 1963. Johnson took the oath of office on board Air Force One in Dallas before returning to Washington, D. C.

Images on television showed the people of the U.S. the true horror of what was happening in Vietnam, and the war became very unpopular.

169

Bill Clinton with his wife, Hillary, and their daughter, Chelsea.

What was Whitewater?

In 1993, people said that money had been illegally given to the Whitewater Land Development Corporation. President Bill Clinton and the first lady, Hillary Clinton, were part owners of the company at the time and were therefore involved in the case.

Which president had too much of his own way?
Andrew Jackson. In 1834, he was told off by the Senate for "dictatorial and unconstitutional behavior" after he took government money from the Bank of America and put it in smaller state banks.

What is impeachment?
Impeachment is the process of bringing legal charges against the president. The Senate acts as a court of law and tries the president.

What was the Iran-Contra scandal?
When Ronald Reagan was president, it was discovered that government officials had secretly been selling weapons to Iran. They used the profits from the sales to help Contra rebels in Nicaragua, who were fighting against the Communist regime in the country.

What was Watergate?

A POLITICAL SCANDAL THAT HAPPENED IN 1972, WHEN REPUBLICAN RICHARD Nixon was president. Five men were arrested after breaking into the rival Democratic party headquarters in the Watergate building in Washington, D.C., with electronic equipment for tapping telephones. It was found that staff from the White House had planned the break-in and organized a cover-up with Nixon's approval. Nixon resigned in August 1974 because of the scandal.

Has a president ever been impeached?
Yes, but only one. He was 17th president, Andrew Johnson. He was impeached in 1868 for sacking his Secretary of War without the consent of the Senate. He was found not guilty by the Senate.

Who has Congress tried to impeach?
Attempts have been made to impeach three presidents (in addition to Andrew Johnson). They are John Tyler, Richard Nixon, and Bill Clinton.

Whose administration was corrupt?
Warren Harding's. He was president from 1921 to 1923. The worst money scandal during this time was the "Teapot Dome," in which Secretary of the Interior Albert Falls gave companies the right to drill for oil in return for money.

Nixon made his resignation speech on television. In 1974, he was pardoned for his part in the scandal by Gerald Ford.

Who shot President Kennedy?

LEE HARVEY OSWALD ... PROBABLY. PRESIDENT KENNEDY WAS SHOT AND killed while driving in a motorcade through Dallas on November 22, 1963. Lee Harvey Oswald, a former marine and a communist, denied firing the gun, but was shot himself before he could be tried. Many people believe that Oswald was not the killer, or at least he did not act alone.

Who shot Kennedy's killer?

Two days after President Kennedy was killed, Lee Harvey Oswald was shot at point-blank range by night-club owner Jack Ruby. Oswald was being moved to prison at the time.

What happens if a president dies in office?

The vice-president is immediately sworn in as president. The new president then selects a new vice-president.

Nobody really knows who Jack Ruby was and why he killed Lee Harvey Oswald, but there are many theories.

Is there a new election after a president's death?

No. The vice-president is elected in partnership with the president, and voters know that he could become president. He serves for the remainder of the presidential term.

Were any other presidents assassinated?

James Garfield and William McKinley. Garfield was shot on July 2, 1881, at Baltimore and Potomac station in Washington, D.C. He died two months later from blood poisoning caused by operations to remove the bullet. McKinley was shot on September 6, 1901, and died eight days later from gangrene.

Has a president been shot and survived?

Yes. Two in fact—Andrew Jackson and Ronald Reagan. In 1835, a man fired two guns at Jackson, but neither discharged. Jackson was lucky because both weapons were later found to be in working order. In 1981, John Hinckley shot Reagan in the chest. Reagan was lucky to survive.

Just five days after Lincoln's victory in the Civil War, he was murdered.

Which president was shot in a theater?

ABRAHAM LINCOLN, THE 16TH PRESIDENT, ON APRIL 14, 1865, AT FORD'S Theater, Washington, D.C. He died the next day. Lincoln was shot from behind while watching the stage from his box. His assassin, John Wilkes Booth, leapt onto the stage, shouting "The South is avenged!" (He was referring to the Civil War, in which the South was defeated.) Booth was shot and killed resisting arrest two days later.

Which president survived a duel?
Andrew Jackson. In a duel in 1806 with Charles Dickinson, a local lawyer, Jackson was shot in the chest. The bullet was never removed. Dickinson died in the duel.

Which other presidents died in office?
Four presidents died of natural causes. They were William Henry Harrison, Zachary Taylor, Warren G. Harding, and Franklin D. Roosevelt.

What was Ronald Reagan's first job?

From 1932, THE 40TH PRESIDENT WAS A BASEBALL AND FOOTBALL RADIO announcer. In 1937, he got an acting contract and by 1965 he had made more than 50 feature films.

Before he began his political career, Ronald Reagan was an actor. Here he is in 1951, posing with his co-star in the film *Bedtime for Bonzo*.

Who could have been a pro football player?

George Bush. As a senior at the University of Michigan, he was named Most Valuable Player on the Michigan Wolverines football team. In 1935, he played for the College All-Stars team against the Chicago Bears. Soon afterward, both the Detroit Lions and Green Bay Packers offered him contracts.

Who overcame a learning disability?

Woodrow Wilson, who at nine years old could still not read or do his arithmetic. He also had bad eyesight and poor health. But he was a great success at college.

Since he was defeated by Reagan in the 1980 election, Carter has been heavily involved in promoting human rights issues.

Which president dressed to impress?

Martin Van Buren. He had a small, solid figure, a balding head with long white hair, and flowing sideburns. He was always perfectly dressed, and was once described as "exquisite in appearance." Van Buren was often criticized in the newspapers for being too interested in what he wore.

Who refused to lie about a cherry tree?

George Washington—but the story is probably a myth. It was claimed that as a child Washington owned up to cutting down his father's cherry tree, saying that he could not tell a lie.

Where did Theodore Roosevelt work for the police?

In New York City. From 1895 to 1897, Roosevelt served as president of the New York City Police Board. He rooted out corruption and enforced a ban on the sale of alcohol on Sundays.

Who sent food to Belgium?

Herbert Hoover, who was head of the American Relief Committee and the Commission for the Relief of Belgium after World War I. He sent 34 million tons of food, clothes and supplies to the people of Europe.

Who worked as a translator aged just 14?

John Quincy Adams, who was president from 1825—1829. He lived in Europe as a child and by the age of 14 he could speak fluent French. He was chosen as secretary to an American politician working in St. Petersburg, Russia.

Which president grew peanuts?

JIMMY CARTER, WHOSE FAMILY RAN A PEANUT FARM IN GEORGIA. CARTER TOOK over the business after the death of his father in 1953. Before this, he was a submarine officer.

General Taylor had little formal education, but was a well-respected soldier. He was only in office for 16 months.

Who made a lucky escape from the French?

During the French and Indian War (1753—1760), George Washington fought in the Virginia Militia. At Pittsburgh, four bullets went through his clothes and two horses were killed as he rode them.

Who won the Battle of New Orleans?

Andrew Jackson. During the War of 1812 (1812—1815), Jackson's troops defended the city against highly-trained British troops. Two thousand British troops were killed or injured, compared to just 21 Americans.

Who led the Union army in the Civil War?

Ulysses S. Grant. In 1862, he won the first major victory of the war against the Confederates, and was promoted to major general. After more victories he was made commander of all the Union armies in 1864.

Who made his name fighting Mexicans?

ZACHARY TAYLOR, WHO FOUGHT IN THE MEXICAN WAR (1846—1848). IN 1847, at Buena Vista, General Taylor's men fought and beat a much larger force of Mexicans. During the battle, two bullets went through Taylor's clothing. Taylor became a hero when news of the victory reached Washington. He later became the 12th president.

Who rode rough at Kettle Hill?

The Rough Riders was a cavalry regiment made up of volunteers. They were formed in 1898 to fight in the Spanish-American War. At Kettle Hill, Cuba, they made a brave charge, led by Colonel Theodore Roosevelt.

Who was the youngest pilot in the navy?

In 1943, George Bush earned his wings to become the youngest pilot in the navy. He flew 58 sorties in torpedo bombers against Japanese ships in the Pacific. He was shot down twice at sea, and won the Distinguished Flying Cross.

What did Eisenhower plan in Europe?

DWIGHT D. EISENHOWER JOINED THE ARMY DURING WORLD WAR I AND SERVED until 1948. In 1943, during World War II, he became a general and was given the title of Supreme Allied Commander. He was ordered to plan Operation Overlord, the Allied invasion of Europe, which began with the D-day landings in France on June 6, 1944.

Why did Kennedy get a Purple Heart?

John F. Kennedy was commander of a patrol boat that was sliced in two by a Japanese destroyer in World War II. He swam to an island, towing an injured crewman with him. He was awarded a Purple Heart medal for bravery.

Who beat the Shawnee Indians at Tippecanoe?

The Battle of Tippecanoe Creek took place in 1811. William Henry Harrison, then Governor of Indiana, with a force of army regulars and militiamen fought off a surprise attack by 700 Shawnees.

After military success in World War II, as president, Eisenhower used his skills to try to solve the Cold War situation.

What did 70 million people watch?

THE FIRST TELEVISED ELECTION DEBATE BETWEEN JOHN F. KENNEDY AND RICHARD Nixon, who were opponents in the 1960 presidential election campaign. They appeared together on four live television debates. An incredible 70 million people watched the first debate.

Who had a tough job in Great Britain?

John Adams was appointed ambassador to Britain in 1785, just two years after America's independence was recognized. It was a tough job because he was the first ambassador, and there were still bad feelings between the countries. Adams returned to the United States in 1788, soon to be elected vice-president.

James Polk may have been little known, but he was said to have brought about the Mexican War with his aggressive policies.

Who asked, "Who is James Polk?"

WHEN THE DEMOCRATS TRIED TO CHOOSE THEIR MAN for the 1844 presidential election, they found it impossible to decide between the candidates. Then James K. Polk entered the race and won. He was so little known that during the elections, members of the Whig party made fun of him, asking, "Who is James Polk?"

The idea of two politicians debating on television caught the imagination of the U.S.

Which rich man pretended to live in a log cabin?
So that people would vote for him, William Henry Harrison's supporters portrayed him as a man of few means, who lived in a small log cabin and drank cheap cider. In fact, he lived in luxury in a 22-room manor house.

Who were the mugwumps?
Mugwumps were Republicans who deserted their own candidate James Blaine to help the campaign of Democrat Grover Cleveland, who was elected president in 1884.

Have all presidents been either Republicans or Democrats?
No. The Federalist party was supported by the first two presidents, George Washington and John Adams. In the mid-1800s, the Whigs had four presidents—William Henry Harrison, John Tyler, Zachary Taylor, and Millard Fillmore.

When was the Republican Party founded?
In 1854. Its first president was Abraham Lincoln. Between 1860 and 1928 all but two presidents were Republicans.

... and the Democratic Party?
The Democratic party was formed in the 1790s. Confusingly, its members called themselves Republicans at first.

Who was the brains behind the Brains Trust?
The Brains Trust was a team of top advisors gathered together by Franklin D. Roosevelt. It helped him to win the 1932 election.

Which first lady is most famous?

Jackie Kennedy, later Onassis, was always in the media spotlight. She was a glamorous woman who was loved by the people of the U.S.

It MUST BE JACQUELINE LEE BOUVIER (1929—1994), WHO BECAME MRS. KENNEDY. She met John F. Kennedy in 1951, and they were married in 1953. After her husband's assassination, she married Greek shipping tycoon Aristotle Onassis in 1968.

When did a dog help a president?

While Richard Nixon was running for vice-president in 1952, he had to defend himself against a charge of accepting gifts of money while he was a senator. On television he gained public support by admitting to receiving just one gift—a dog named Checkers.

Who was born at an inn?

Andrew Johnson was born in the winter of 1808 in a log cabin in the grounds of an inn, where his father worked as a porter. He grew up in extreme poverty.

Which presidents were related?

Three sets of presidents have been related. John Quincy Adams was one of four children of John Adams. Benjamin Harrison was one of 13 children of John Scott Harrison, who was one of nine children of William Henry Harrison. Theodore Roosevelt was a fifth cousin of Franklin D. Roosevelt.

Who was the first poor president?

The first six presidents all came from well-off families. The father of the seventh, Andrew Jackson, was a poor farmer who had emigrated to the United States from Ireland.

Which president married his cousin?

In 1905, Franklin D. Roosevelt married Eleanor Roosevelt, his fifth cousin, once removed. She took an active part in politics, and after her husband's death she served as Chair of the United Nations Commission on Human Rights.

Which presidential family is most famous?

In modern times, it must be the Kennedys. John F. Kennedy's father, Joseph Patrick Kennedy, was a millionaire businessman by the age of 35. Two of his brothers entered politics. Robert F. Kennedy was attorney general and a senator. He was assassinated in 1968. Edward Kennedy was also a senator.

Who married a rich widow?

In 1659, George Washington married Martha Dandridge Custis, a widow with a large estate known as White House (not the White House). She was said to be the wealthiest widow in Virginia. In 1752, he inherited another fortune, his brother's large estate, called Mount Vernon.

What did the S. in Harry S. Truman stand for?

NOTHING! S. WAS HIS MIDDLE NAME! TRUMAN'S PARENTS COULD NOT DECIDE between the names Shippe or Solomon, the names of his two grandfathers, so they left it as simply S. instead.

Harry Truman came from a farming background. He became president when Roosevelt died in 1945.

Who was married twice—to the same wife?

Andrew Jackson. In 1791 he married Rachel Donelson Robards. But the marriage was not legal because Rachel was not divorced from her first husband. They were remarried (properly this time) in 1794.

Calvin Coolidge believed in not interfering with the United States' business. He was also known to be sincere.

Who advised counting to 10?

Thomas Jefferson, the 3rd president of the United States. In his book entitled *A Decalogue of Canons for Observation in Practical Life* he wrote: "When angry, count to 10 before you speak; if very angry, a hundred."

What did Lincoln say about fooling people?

"You may fool all the people some of the time; you can even fool some of the people all the time; but you can't fool all of the people all the time."

How did Washington keep the peace?

In his first speech to the American Congress, in 1790, President Washington said, "To be prepared for war is one of the most effectual means of preserving peace."

George Bush was head of the CIA in 1976—7. He is best-known for taking the U.S. into the Gulf War.

Which president was really cool?

CALVIN COOLIDGE. "KEEP COOL WITH COOLIDGE" WAS THE SLOGAN USED BY the Republicans during the 1924 presidential election campaign.

Who advised carrying a big stick?

President Theodore Roosevelt's motto was, "Speak softly and carry a big stick; you will go far." He meant that you should use diplomacy, but be ready to use force if necessary.

What did Wilson encourage fools to do?

Speak! In a speech in 1919, President Wilson said, "If a man is a fool, the best thing to do is to encourage him to advertise the fact by speaking."

What was Kennedy's most famous saying?

In his inaugural address in 1961, John F. Kennedy said: "And so, my fellow Americans: Ask not what your country can do for you—ask what you can do for your country."

**What was the
Gettysburg Address?**
It was a speech made by President
Abraham Lincoln at the site of the
Battle of Gettysburg,
Pennsylvania, on November 19,
1863, just after the Civil War
ended. It contained just 286
words, yet it is one of the most
famous speeches ever made. In it,
Lincoln spoke of "Government of
the people, by the people, and for
the people."

Who wanted his lips read?

GEORGE BUSH. DURING THE
PRESIDENTIAL ELECTION CAMPAIGN IN 1988
he announced: "Read my lips: No new taxes." He was
reminded of this when several taxes were raised in 1990.

Whose heads are carved into a mountain?

FOUR OF THE GREATEST AMERICAN PRESIDENTS ARE REMEMBERED AT MOUNT Rushmore National Memorial in South Dakota. Huge heads of George Washington, Thomas Jefferson, Abraham Lincoln, and Theodore Roosevelt are carved into the granite of Mount Rushmore. Carving started in 1927 and finished in 1941.

Whose monument stands close to the White House?
The Washington Monument, dedicated to President George Washington. It is an obelisk 555 ft (170 m) high, with a square base. It was built between 1848 and 1884. Visitors can take an elevator to the top.

Gutzon Borglum did most of the carving at Mount Rushmore, but when he died in 1941 his son took over.

Which president is remembered at an airport?
John F. Kennedy International Airport, New York City, was named after President Kennedy. John F. Kennedy Airport, in Dallas-Fort Worth is also named after him.

Why are bears called teddies?
Theodore Roosevelt's nickname was Teddy. In 1902, while on a hunting trip in Mississippi, he refused to shoot a bear cub. This inspired a famous cartoon, which in turn inspired a toy called Teddy's bear.

Who was known as His Accidency?
John Tyler. He was vice-president to William Henry Harrison. When President Harrison died suddenly, Tyler took over. His opponents did not think he should be president, and called him His Accidency.

Which president holds back water?
In 1947, the Boulder Dam on the Colorado River was renamed the Hoover Dam to honor President Herbert Hoover. At 726 ft (221 m) high, it is the highest concrete arch dam in the United States.

Who was General Mum?
William Henry Harrison. The name was given to him because he stayed mum (quiet) during the election campaign. He won because of the way his supporters criticized his opponent, Martin Van Buren.

Who is sculpted in bronze?
Thomas Jefferson, the 3rd president and the man who drafted the Declaration of Independence. The Thomas Jefferson Memorial in Washington, D.C. is a classical monument with a bronze figure of Jefferson.

Who was Old Man Eloquent?
John Quincy Adams. He earned the nickname after retiring as president and returning to Congress in the House of Representatives, where he served for 17 years.

Which president was never afraid?
President Lyndon B. Johnson said of Franklin D. Roosevelt, "He was the one person I ever knew, anywhere, who was never afraid."

The Hoover Dam provides water for southern California, Arizona, and Mexico.

Sporting Heroes

Who was the "father of football"?

WALTER CAMP, A PLAYER AND coach at Yale. In the 1880s, he introduced many of the rules that are still used in the modern game. These included a system for scoring points, a team of 11 instead of 15 (as in rugby), the quarterback position, the line of scrimmage, and the idea that a team had to give up the ball if they did not advance by enough yards after a number of downs.

Walter Camp followed a strict regime of physical training, and self denial and was an oustanding all-round athlete.

What are the Queensberry Rules?
They are 12 rules of modern boxing, written in 1867 by John Graham Chambers and named after the Marquis of Queensberry. They introduced three-minute rounds, one-minute rests, the ten-second count, and gloves.

What are "All-American" teams?
All-American teams are picked at the end of each season to indicate which college players have performed best in which position. The idea was pioneered by Walter Camp, who announced the first All-American football teams in 1889.

188

Who invented lacrosse?

Lacrosse was invented by Native Americans in Canada, who called it "baggataway." Games played by the Iroquois tribe could last three days. There were up to 1,000 players on each team, and one of the aims was to disable as many of your opponents as possible. A modern version became the national sport of Canada and was introduced to the U.S. in 1868.

Who umpired and made the rules for the first real game of baseball?

A New York City surveyor named Alexander J. Cartwright developed 20 rules. In 1846, he umpired the first game using nine-player teams and a diamond with four bases. Fielders could run a batter out by tagging him, instead of by throwing the ball at him, as in the British game of cricket.

How was the first basketball game played?

It was played using a soccer ball, with two peach buckets nailed to the walls of a YMCA gym. A ladder was used to retrieve the ball after a basket was scored. It was invented by Canadian James Naismith in 1891.

What did John Reid and six friends form in 1888?

They formed the United States' first golf club, St. Andrews, using a three-hole course in a New York cow pasture. The first member was Robert Lockhart, a linen merchant who had brought the clubs and balls back from Scotland.

When was the first great international boxing match?

It was fought with bare knuckles on April 17, 1860, between John C. Heenan of the U.S. and English champion Tom Sayers. The referee vanished when the crowd stormed the ring, and after 42 rounds it was called a draw.

Abner Doubleday is said to have devised the present-day playing positions of baseball.

Who was Abner Doubleday?

ACCORDING TO LEGEND, ARMY CADET DOUBLEDAY INVENTED BASEBALL in the summer of 1839, in a cow field in Cooperstown, New York. This is why the Baseball Hall of Fame was built there. In fact, the game played by Doubleday was more like the English game of rounders.

Who was the "Boston Strong Boy"?

Tʜᴇ GREAT JOHN L. SULLIVAN, WHO BECAME THE LAST World Heavyweight Boxing Champion of the bare-knuckle era by knocking out Paddy Ryan in nine rounds in 1882. He once won a 75-round fight in temperatures of up to 104°F (40°C). He was the first sporting hero to be paid to advertise products, and earned over $1 million during his career. Sport magazine called him: "A hero among heroes."

Who was the first professional football player?

William "Pudge" Heffelfinger became the first professional football player when Allegheny Athletic Club paid him $500 to join them. Playing as a guard for Yale, he had been picked for the All-American teams for the previous three years.

Did Heffelfinger enjoy football?

It would appear so. Heffelfinger was the first blocker to protect the ballcarrier by providing "interference." He spoke of "the fierce elation that comes from throwing your body across an opponent's knees and feeling him hit the turf with a solid crack."

John L. Sullivan knocked Paddy Ryan out in the 9th round of the World Heavyweight Championship of 1882 in less than 11 minutes.

When did baseball's Major Leagues begin?

Baseball's National League was founded in 1876. In 1900, the Western League was renamed the American League by its president, Ban Johnson. These two leagues became the Major Leagues.

How did Walker Breeze Smith win one of the United States' first golf matches?

He told his opponent, John C. Ten Eyck, that the secret was to keep your eye on the ball. He then promptly removed his glass eye, balanced it on the ball, and teed off.

When was the first U.S. Open Golf Championship?

The first U.S. Open was played in 1895. When Fred Herd won the trophy in 1898, the United States Golf Association made him put down a deposit for the trophy. Golfers had such a bad reputation at that time, that they thought he might pawn it!

What did Harry Decker invent?

Decker was the inventor of the padded catcher's glove used in baseball. These gloves were known as "deckers" for many years.

How did the Civil War affect baseball?

During the Civil War, Union soldiers from New York City played the game wherever the fighting took them. In this way, they spread the rules used by the first real team—Alexander Cartwright's New York Knickerbocker Baseball Club.

Who was baseball's first legend?

CAP ANSON, WHO MADE HIS DEBUT IN THE NEW NATIONAL LEAGUE for the Chicago White Stockings (now white sox) in 1876. He was the first player to make 3,000 hits, and played professional baseball for 27 years. A candy bar and a cigarette were named after him, and a reporter wrote, "He stood at first base like a mighty oak ... the symbol of all that was strong and good in baseball."

Adrian C. "Cap" Anson played in first base from 1879.

Which hero of baseball made his debut in 1890?

CY YOUNG, WHO MANY CONSIDER TO BE THE greatest pitcher ever, made his debut for Cleveland. Born Denton True Young, in Ohio, he went on to win an all-time record 511 Major League games during his career.

Cy Young claimed never to have been sick until he caught the flu at the age of 79.

Why did James Connolly almost not win his Olympic medal?
He misunderstood the Greek calendar during the 1896 Olympics in Athens, Greece, and stayed up celebrating for the whole night before his historic track and field event.

What did James B. Connolly receive in 1896?
Connolly received the first Olympic winner's medal awarded since Barasdates of Greece won the boxing in AD 393. The Olympics were revived at Athens in 1896 by Frenchman Baron Pierre de Coubertin, after a gap of 1,503 years. A triple jumper from Harvard, Connolly received a silver medal for winning. Gold was considered vulgar, and was not used for winner's medals until 1904.

Gentleman Jim beat John L. Sullivan in 1892 for a purse of $25,000.

Which great jockey invented the crouching position used by jockeys today?

Tod Sloan, from Indiana, invented the "monkey crouch." It was more comfortable for him to ride with short stirrups and his head almost on the horse's neck, because he had incredibly short legs.

Why was baseball's pitching mound moved from 50 ft (15 m) to 60 ft, 6 in (18.5 m) from the batter?

Because pitcher Rusie Amos, the "Hoosier Thunderbolt," pitched so fast that it was unfair on the batters. His catcher had to wear a sheet of lead in his glove.

How did Jim Corbett change boxing?

He was known as the "father of scientific boxing" for his skill inside the ring. He was also nicknamed the "California Dandy" for his elegant appearance outside the ring. Both of these qualities helped to make boxing popular with the public.

What did Dr. Coburn Haskell invent in 1898?

Haskell, a dentist from Cleveland, was playing with a bundle of rubber bands when his idea struck him. He invented a golf ball, filled with twisted rubber bands, so it flew much further than previous balls.

How did professional basketball develop?

The National Basketball League (NBL) was formed in 1898. It started as an attempt to find opponents who could take on the brilliant Trenton team of the YMCA League.

What did "Gentleman Jim" win in 1892?

"GENTLEMAN JIM" CORBETT KNOCKED OUT JOHN L. SULLIVAN IN NEW Orleans to win the first World Heavyweight Championship fought with gloves under Queensberry rules. Sullivan was unfit, but was not knocked out until the 21st round.

Who started the search for the "Great White Hope"?

The "Galveston Giant" Jack Johnson, who became the first black World Heavyweight Champion by knocking out Tommy Burns in Sydney, Australia, in 1908. Johnson upset white society by hiring servants, buying a fleet of luxury cars, and twice marrying white women. So a desperate search for a white boxer—a "Great White Hope"—who might beat him began. Nobody succeeded until 1915.

How did President Roosevelt change the shape of football?

In 1905, President Roosevelt insisted that a bone-breaking, battering-ram formation called the "flying wedge" should be banned from the game. He did it after 18 players were killed in the previous season!

President Roosevelt was a great football fan.

What did May Sutton wear to cause trouble at Wimbledon?

In 1905, because she was only 18, May Sutton was allowed to wear a dress that did not cover up her ankles. This glimpse of the Californian youngster's legs caused a lot of trouble at the All-England Club. Her tennis also upset the British, as she went on to become the first non-English player to win Wimbledon.

Why did Jack Johnson flee from the U.S. in 1912?

He had been convicted of breaking a law by crossing state lines with his wife before they were married. Johnson fled, disguised as a member of a black baseball team, and defended his title abroad.

Who won the first World Series?

The first World Series was played in 1903, between the winners of the National League and the new American League. Cy Young pitched the Boston Red Sox to a 5—3 victory over Pittsburgh.

Why was Cy Young perfect in 1904?

He pitched the first ever perfect game in baseball history, playing for the Boston Red Sox against the Philadelphia Athletics. Not a single Philadelphia batter reached first base on either a hit or a walk.

How did Charles Follis become the first black professional football player?

Follis agreed to join the Shelby team in exchange for being given a job in a hardware store in 1904. He became known as the "Black Cyclone," and was a major star of the Ohio League.

Which Olympic champion was punched for jumping on a Sunday?

Alvin Kranzlein won his fourth gold medal with a record-breaking long jump at the 1904 Paris Olympics in France. Previous record-holder Meyer Prinstein, who had refused to compete because the event was on a Sunday, ran up and socked him!

Who won a famous marathon by coming second?

Johnny Hayes, a sales clerk at Bloomingdales, finished 0.75 seconds behind Italian Dorando Pietri in the marathon at the London Olympics of 1908 in England. But Pietri was disqualified, because British officials had carried him over the line after he collapsed!

Who appears on the most valuable baseball card?

Honus Wagner, the great Pittsburgh shortstop who led the league in batting for eight seasons from 1900 to 1911. The 1909 card bearing his image was withdrawn because Wagner, who was against smoking, thought it set a bad example for children to see the cards in packs of cigarettes.

Honus Wagner once said, "There isn't much to being a ballplayer, if you're a ballplayer."

Why did Ty Cobb keep a gun beside his bed?
Cobb's heroes were the aggressive rulers Napoleon and Caesar, and he ruled in a similar way on the baseball park. He upset so many players that he needed the gun to protect himself from his own teammates!

Which Native American won two Olympic golds?

JIM THORPE, WHOSE NATIVE AMERICAN NAME WAS WA-THO-HUCK, meaning "Bright Path." He followed a very bright path at the 1912 Stockholm Olympics, setting records in the Decathlon and Pentathlon. King Gustav of Sweden told him: "You are the greatest athlete in the world," to which Thorpe replied: "Thanks, King!" Thorpe's medals were tragically taken back because he had been paid $2 a game to play baseball—and was therefore not an amateur.

Jim Thorpe was voted outstanding male athlete of the first 50 years of the last century.

Who was the "Georgia Peach"?
This was the nickname of Ty Cobb, one of the most feared and ferocious players ever. Cobb played 22 seasons with the Detroit Tigers of the American League. He led the league in batting for nine consecutive years from 1907 to 1915, and has the all-time best batting average (.367). His aggressive style was shown in his career total of 892 stolen bases, a record which lasted until 1979.

What did Marshall Foch say about football?

Marshall Foch, the Frenchman who commanded the Allied Forces during World War I, said of a football game between the Army and Navy—"Mon Dieu, this game is war! It has everything."

What was the "Battle of the Camera Shot"?

The fight in which Jack Johnson was defeated by Jess Willard in 1915. Johnson claimed that a camera shot of him shading his eyes from the Sun after his knockout proved that he had lost the fight deliberately and had not really been knocked out.

What scandal shocked baseball fans in 1919?

The "Black Sox" scandal. After the Chicago White Sox lost the 1919 World Series to the Cincinatti Reds, eight players were accused of throwing the game for gamblers' money. They were acquitted, but were banned for life anyway.

Which shop assistant started a popular golfing boom?

Francis Ouimet, who in 1913 became the first amateur to win the U.S. Open. He beat famous British professionals Harry Vardon and Ted Ray in a play-off. His caddy was only 10 years old!

Who became a football legend in only four years?

George Gipp, fullback for the famous Notre Dame college team. He became a national celebrity in a four-year career (1917—1920). He died, at the age of 25, after playing a game while sick with a temperature of 102°F (39°C).

"Shoeless" Joe Jackson was one of the best hitters ever in baseball.

Who was "Shoeless" Joe Jackson?

A GREAT HITTER, WHO ONCE PLAYED IN SOCKS BECAUSE HIS NEW SHOES GAVE him blisters. He was the most popular player banned in the Black Sox scandal, causing the public to cry— "Say it ain't so, Joe!"

Who was Babe Ruth?

GEORGE HERMAN RUTH, FROM

Baltimore, known as "Babe" and the "Sultan of Swat" was baseball's biggest-ever hero. A huge slugger, he shattered every batting record. His lifetime 714 home runs was not beaten until 1974, and his 60 homers in one season (1927) set one of sport's most famous records. Amazingly, he began his career as a pitcher. Even then, he set a World Series record of 29 scoreless innings for the Boston Red Sox.

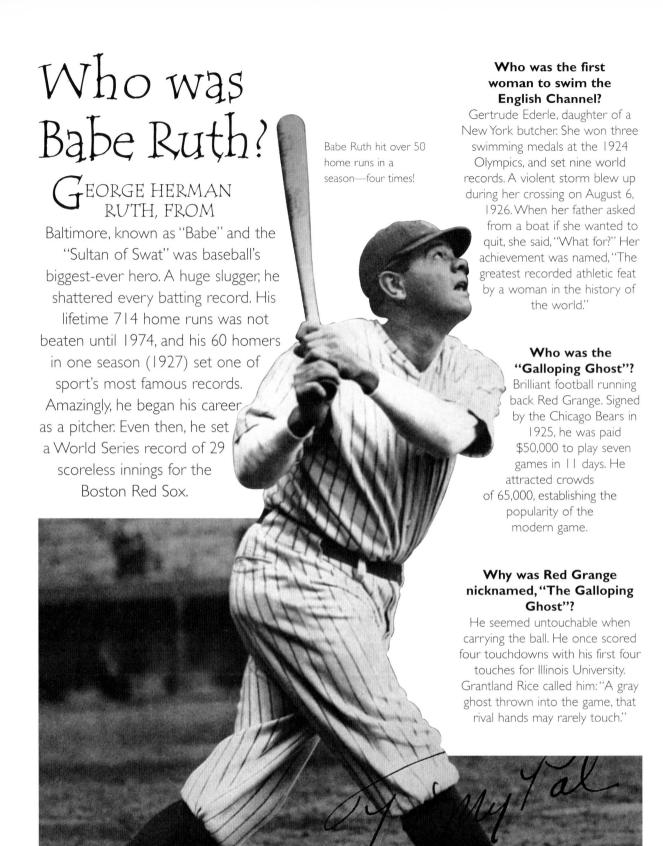

Babe Ruth hit over 50 home runs in a season—four times!

Who was the first woman to swim the English Channel?

Gertrude Ederle, daughter of a New York butcher. She won three swimming medals at the 1924 Olympics, and set nine world records. A violent storm blew up during her crossing on August 6, 1926. When her father asked from a boat if she wanted to quit, she said, "What for?" Her achievement was named, "The greatest recorded athletic feat by a woman in the history of the world."

Who was the "Galloping Ghost"?

Brilliant football running back Red Grange. Signed by the Chicago Bears in 1925, he was paid $50,000 to play seven games in 11 days. He attracted crowds of 65,000, establishing the popularity of the modern game.

Why was Red Grange nicknamed, "The Galloping Ghost"?

He seemed untouchable when carrying the ball. He once scored four touchdowns with his first four touches for Illinois University. Grantland Rice called him: "A gray ghost thrown into the game, that rival hands may rarely touch."

Helen Wills won gold medals in both singles and doubles tennis at the 1924 Olympic Games.

Who was "Little Miss Poker Face"?

Helen Wills, who was named for her

serious approach to tennis. It seemed to work. She did not drop a set between 1927 and 1932, and in her career she won seven U.S. titles and eight Wimbledons.

What was Walter Hagen's catchphrase?
"Don't hurry, don't worry, you're here only a short time, so be sure to smell the flowers." Hagen, who often played in the previous night's dinner suit, became golf's first millionaire by winning ten majors.

Why was Tarzan such a good swimmer?
In 19 movies of the 1930s, the role of Tarzan was played by Johnny Weissmüller. He had won three swimming golds at the 1924 Paris Olympics, and two more in 1928, and broke 67 world amateur records.

Why did the Harlem Globetrotters "globetrot"?
They had no court, so they traveled the U.S. in promoter Abe Saperstein's car. They started as a competitive side in 1927, but became a world-touring exhibition side. No black players were allowed in the NBA until 1950.

What law did heavyweight champ Jack Dempsey necessitate?
The rule saying a boxer has to retire to a neutral corner after a knockdown was introduced after Dempsey, the "Manassa Mauler", repeatedly knocked down Luis Firpo in a brutal 1923 fight.

What did Mildred "Babe" Didrikson achieve?

THIS AMAZING TEXAN

won the gold and set world records in the javelin and 80 meters hurdles at the 1932 Los Angeles Olympics. She

Mildred Didrikson was nicknamed "Babe" after hitting 13 home runs against a boys team.

received the silver in the high jump because her "western roll" style was judged illegal! She played on three championship basketball teams, toured playing billiards, and once pitched out Joe DiMaggio. Didrikson later helped establish the women's golf tour, winning the Women's U.S. title three times.

Why did President Roosevelt squeeze Joe Louis' biceps?
In 1938, Louis was fighting German champion Max Schmeling. With war looming, Roosevelt told him, "We need muscles like yours to beat Germany." Louis won in one round.

Who was the first sportsman to have a bigger salary than the President?
Babe Ruth, who received $80,000 for the 1930 season. When asked why he deserved to earn more money than the President, Ruth said, "I had a better year!"

Who held the World Heavyweight Boxing title for the longest time?
The brilliant "Brown Bomber" Joe Louis. He won the title from James Braddock in 1937, and held it for 11 years, 8 months. He defended 25 times, against a series of "Bum of the Month" challengers.

Owen's long jump record was unbroken for 25 years, 79 days.

How long did it take Jesse Owens to set four world records?

About 45 minutes. Between 3:15 and 4:00 p.m. on May 25 1935, representing Ohio University, Owens set records in the 100 yards, 220 yards, 220 yard hurdles, and running broad jump.

What baseball record did Lou Gehrig set?

Between June 1, 1925 and May 2, 1939, the "Iron Horse" played 2,130 consecutive games for the New York Yankees. He ignored broken fingers and pulled muscles to set a record that lasted until 1995.

What was the first object placed in baseball's Hall of Fame?

When the Hall of Fame opened in 1936, the spikes of Ty Cobb, the first elected member, were put on display. Cobb sharpened his spikes so that he could leave fielders a reminder of his presence.

Which golfer won the "Impossible Quadrilateral"?

In 1930, Bobby Jones became the only golfer ever to win the old Grand Slam—or "Impossible Quadrilateral" as it was called—of U.S. Amateur, U.S. Open, British Amateur, and British Open titles of one year.

Was Bronco Nagurski the toughest football player ever?

Possibly. The Chicago Bears fullback (1930—1937) once bulldozed through opponents for a 45-yard touchdown, collided with the goalposts, and ran on into a brick wall. Regaining consciousness, he said, "That last guy hit me awfully hard."

How was Hitler taught a lesson at the 1936 Berlin Olympics?

HITLER HAD HOPED WHITE ATHLETES WOULD DEMONSTRATE THEIR

racial supremacy. Black American athlete Jesse Owens, the 22-year-old son of cotton picker, had other ideas. He broke three Olympic records and equaled another in winning gold in the 100 meters, 200 meters, long jump and 4 x 100 meters relay. Hitler refused to present the medals. Owens remarked, "We lost no sleep over not being greeted by Adolf Hitler."

Joe DiMaggio (shown left of Mickey Mantle) was known for his graceful style.

How did the war affect sporting heroes?

Baseball stars enlisted, and the All-Star game was cancelled in 1945. Some football teams stopped playing. The Pittsburgh Steelers and Philadelphia Eagles merged as the "Steagles" for one season. Hockey overtime was banned. More women and black players became stars.

What was the lace panties scandal?

In 1949, "Gorgeous Gussy" Moran from California shocked Wimbledon by wearing a lace trim beneath a shorter than usual skirt. Designer Ted Tinling had to resign from his post as a Wimbledon official, but became famous as a dress designer.

Which golfing legend failed to win the U.S. Open?

Sam Snead won the 1946 British Open, three PGAs, and three Masters but could never win the US Open. He was runner-up four times, and in 1947 missed a 30-inch putt on the last hole.

Who was football's "Papa Bear"?

George Halas, who coached the Chicago Bears to a record 320 wins. In 1940, they scored a record NFL Championship victory of 73—0 against the Washington Redskins. At 66—0 they were asked not to convert a touchdown, because they had run out of balls!

What did Simon and Garfunkel sing about Joe DiMaggio?

In the 1968 song *Mrs Robinson*, they sang, "Where have you gone, Joe DiMaggio? / A nation turns its lonely eyes to you / What's that you say, Mrs. Robinson? / "Joltin" Joe has left and gone away."

Which baseball legend married Marilyn Monroe?

"JOLTIN" JOE DIMAGGIO, THE "YANKEE CLIPPER," A LEGENDARY SLUGGER and fielder. In 1941, he hit safely in a record 56 straight games—a run that almost ended when his brother nearly caught him! This winning streak led to one of the nine World Series DiMaggio won with the New York Yankees. He married fellow legend Marilyn Monroe in 1954, but they divorced a short time later.

Who was baseball's oldest-ever Major League rookie?

Satchell Paige, who was signed from the Negro Leagues by the Cleveland Indians in 1948, age 42. A crowd of 72,000 watched his debut, and he went on to pitch in the Major League at the age of 59.

How did Sugar Ray Robinson get his name?

WALKER SMITH JR. BORROWED AN IDENTITY CARD FROM HIS friend, Ray Robinson, so he could fight when under-age. He was called "sweet as sugar." As "Sugar Ray Robinson" he was possibly the greatest boxer of all time.

What was the color barrier in baseball?

Black players were only allowed to play in the Negro Leagues, never in the Major Leagues. The unfairness of this situation became even clearer when black soldiers fought for the United States in World War II. The sporting hero who broke this barrier was Jackie Robinson, when he signed for the Brooklyn Dodgers in 1947. He won the first Rookie of the Year award, despite some white players refusing to play against him.

From 1943—51 Sugar Ray Robinson won 91 consecutive fights.

Who was the first black woman to win Wimbledon?

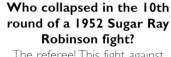

ALTHEA GIBSON, WHO WON THE TITLE IN 1957. GIBSON'S TALENT HAD BEEN spotted as a 13-year-old by the Police Athletic Supervisor, who bought her two secondhand rackets. She impressed U.S. tournaments, where campaigns had to be staged to allow black players to compete. In her career, Gibson won two Wimbledons, two U.S. Championships, and one French title.

Who collapsed in the 10th round of a 1952 Sugar Ray Robinson fight?
The referee! This fight against Joey Maxim at Yankee Stadium for the light-heavyweight championship was the only one in which Robinson was ever stopped. He retired with heat exhaustion in the 13th round.

Why did Ben Hogan offer to get his lawnmower?
Golf's "Ice Man" won one British Open, four U.S. Opens, two PGAs, and two Masters. When he won the British Open at Carnoustie, Scotland, he said of the long grass on the greens, "I've got a lawnmower back in Texas. I'll send it over."

Who was the only unbeaten heavyweight champion?
The "Brockton Blockbuster" Rocky Marciano. He won the title from Jersey Joe Walcott in 1952, and ended his career with 49 wins, 42 knockouts, and 0 losses— despite a short reach that meant he sometimes had to jump to land punches.

How did "Little Mo" get her name?
Big-hitting Maureen Connolly, who won tennis's Grand Slam in 1953, was named after "Big Mo"—the U.S. battleship *Missouri*. She won three U.S. titles and three Wimbledons before injury forced her into retirement at the age of only 19.

Althea Gibson was 30 when she won her first Wimbledon title.

Bill Russell was voted the NBA's Most Valuable Player five times.

What hat-trick did basketball's Bill Russell score in 1956?

In a single year, legendary center Bill Russell led the University of San Francisco to the college championship by winning their last 56 games; led the U.S. to gold at the Melbourne Olympics in Australia, then joined the Boston Celtics mid-season and helped them to the NBA title. Black players had not played in the NBA until 1950. Russell went on to win 11 titles in 13 years with the Celtics, and in 1966 became the NBA's first black coach.

Who was baseball's "Say Hey Kid"?
The legendary Willie Mays of the Giants, who used to address people with "Say, hey!" He hit 660 home runs in his joyous career, and his 460-ft- (140-meter-), over-the-shoulder catch in the 1954 World Series is one of baseball's magic moments.

Who hit the longest home run?
New York Yankees hero Mickey Mantle, who launched a 634-ft (193-meter) homer out of Briggs Stadium, Detroit, against the Detroit Tigers in September 1960. Mantle could hit homers either left-handed or right-handed, and led the league six times in runs.

Which baseball star was the cartoon character Yogi Bear named after?
The New York Yankees catcher Yogi Berra. He won 14 pennants in his 19-year career, and was also famous for making many memorable remarks, including, "It ain't over until it's over."

How successful was Otto Graham?
Graham was the most successful quarterback ever. In his 10-year career from 1946 to 1955, his team, the Cleveland Browns, won a conference title in every season and a league title in seven seasons.

How did Muhammad Ali lose his world heavyweight title?

In 1967, he was stripped of his title for refusing to join US conscription to fight in Vietnam. He said: "I don't have no quarrel with them Vietcongs."

Who lived in a penthouse with llama-fur carpets?

The flamboyant "Broadway" Joe Namath, the first quarterback to pass for 4,000 yards. In 1969, Namath promised that his New York Jets would beat hot favorites the Baltimore Colts in the Superbowl. They did, 16—7.

Did Roger Maris break Babe Ruth's record?

In 1961, Maris broke Ruth's hallowed record of 60 home runs in a season. However, he hit his 61st homer in the 162nd game, while Ruth's season lasted only 154 games. So, many people felt the Babe's record still stood.

Who was "The Greatest"?

MUHAMMAD ALI CLAIMED TO BE "THE GREATEST," AND WENT ON TO BECOME the most famous sportsman on the planet. In 1964, when he was still known as Cassius Clay, he defeated heavyweight champion Sonny Liston, who was believed to be unbeatable. Clay converted to Islam, and adopted his new name. As Muhammad Ali, he lit up sport with his boxing skills, predictions of victory, playful boasting, and famous poems such as his claim that he could, "Float like a butterfly, sting like a bee."

When was the first Superbowl played?

In 1967, after the merger of the National Football League (formed in 1922) and the American Football League (formed 1960). The Green Bay Packers (NFL) beat the Kansas City Chiefs (AFL) 35—10 in the first annual Superbowl between the champions of each league.

After Bob Beamon's record-breaking long jump of over 29 ft (8.9 m), he never again jumped over 27 ft (8 m).

Muhammed Ali won 22 world title fights and lost three.

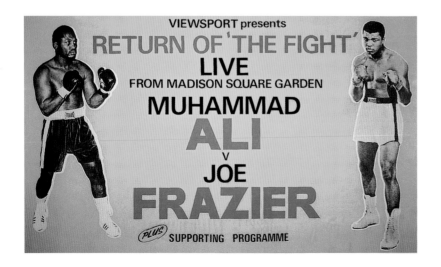

VIEWSPORT presents
RETURN OF 'THE FIGHT'
LIVE
FROM MADISON SQUARE GARDEN
MUHAMMAD
ALI
v
JOE
FRAZIER
PLUS SUPPORTING PROGRAMME

What did Bobby Jones say about Jack Nicklaus?

Jones famously said of "Golden Bear" Nicklaus: "He plays a game with which I am not familiar." Nicklaus, possibly the greatest golfer ever, won three British Open, four U.S., six Masters, and five PGA titles.

What was the "jump into the 21st Century"?

AT THE 1968 MEXICO OLYMPICS, EVERYTHING CAME RIGHT FOR New York City's Bob Beamon. In the final of the long jump, he jumped beyond the gaze of the electronic measuring device. The judges used a tape measure to discover Beamon had leapt 29 feet (8.90 m), beating the world record by an astonishing 22 inches (55 cm). Beamon was so overcome, he collapsed. Another competitor said: "Compared to this jump, the rest of us are children."

What happened to Wilma Rudolph's shoes?

Wilma Rudolph won the gold in the 100 meters, 200 meters, and relay at the 1960 Rome Olympics. As a child, she had needed special shoes because of polio. Then her running shoes were stolen by souvenir hunters.

Who was Wilt the Stilt?

Wilt Chamberlain, the legendary basketball rival of Bill Russell. In 1962, the 7 ft 1 in (2.16 m) center became the first player to score 100 points in a game, for the Philadelphia Warriors. He later became a volleyball superstar.

Who is in the Hall of Fame for both football and lacrosse?

Jim Brown was one of the greatest college lacrosse players ever. He then led football rushing yardages in eight out of nine years for the Cleveland Browns from 1957 to 1965, setting a record for 12,312 yards rushing.

Mark Spitz
swimming butterfly.

What did Mark Spitz achieve at the 1972 Munich Olympics?

THE CALIFORNIAN SWIMMER WON SEVEN GOLD MEDALS AND set seven world records—two in freestyle, two in butterfly, and three in relays. As sport grew more commercial, Spitz retired and made money by appearing in advertisements for clothes, milk, hairdryers, and electric razors. He said of his seven golds, "The medals weighed a lot. They have heavy, crazy chains. Really, it was hard to stand up straight wearing them all."

Which athlete remained unbeaten for an amazing 10 years?

After victory in the World Cup 400 meters hurdles in 1977, Ed Moses won his next 122 races. During this time, he collected Olympic gold at Los Angeles in 1984 and broke the world record four times.

Who presented her opponent with a live pig?

Billie Jean King gave the pig to self-proclaimed male-chauvinist pig Bobby Riggs, before their famous 1973 "Battle of the Sexes" tennis match. An audience of 50 million television viewers watched King defeat ex-pro Riggs. Billie Jean King had helped women's tennis to gain proper recognition by winning an amazing 20 Wimbledon titles during her career: six singles, 10 doubles, four mixed doubles.

Who was known as "The Juice"?

O. J. Simpson, one of the most graceful runningbacks ever. Playing for the Buffalo Bills, he shattered Jim Brown's rushing record, and became the first player to rush for 2,000 yards in a season.

What great baseball record did "Hammering Hank" break?

In 1974, Henry Aaron hit his 715th career home run, overtaking the Babe's 714. The ball he hit it with is now in the Hall of Fame, and Aaron went on to set a career record of 755 homers.

What were the "Rumble in the Jungle" and the "Thrilla in Manilla"?

Two of Muhammad Ali's most famous fights. In the Rumble, in Zaire in 1974, Ali outwitted the enormous George Foreman to regain his title in eight rounds. In the Thrilla in 1975, he defeated Joe Frazier in 15 rounds.

How did Arthur Ashe prepare for his Wimbledon final?

By playing blackjack into the early hours. As a child, Arthur Ashe had been banned from tournaments in Virginia because of his color. In 1975, he beat Jimmy Connors to become the first black player to win the men's singles at Wimbledon.

Which engaged couple won five Grand-Slam tennis events?

IN 1974, 19-YEAR-OLD CHRIS EVERT WON THE FRENCH AND WIMBLEDON titles. Her fiancé, 20-year-old Jimmy Connors, won the Wimbledon, U.S., and Australian titles. They split up at the end of the year.

Why was dunking banned from college basketball in 1968?

To try to reduce the dominance of Lew Alcindor, who led UCLA to three college championships. After changing his name to Kareem Abdul-Jabbar, he broke all scoring records in helping the LA Lakers to five NBA championships.

Who is "Mr Hockey"?

Canadian Gordie Howe, who played 33 seasons of ice hockey, mainly for the Detroit Red Wings. He set the NHL record for points (1,809), won a WHA title playing alongside his two sons, and appeared in his 23rd All-Star game at the age of 51.

Connors was known for his powerful return of serve, Evert for her steady baseline play.

Who is the highest-rated quarterback ever?

JOE MONTANA, WHO WAS NAMED MVP IN THE NFL FOUR TIMES. HE MADE the San Francisco 49ers the team of the 80s, winning four Superbowls between 1982 and 1990. In the Championship game of 1982, he threw a famous play known as "The Catch". With a minute to play, losing 21—17, he threw a high pass to Dwight Clark for a touchdown. Montana said: "I don't know how he got it. He can't jump that high!"

Which ice hockey records does Wayne Gretsky hold?

Known simply as "The Great One," Gretsky dominated his sport more than any other team player in history. Playing for the Edmonton Oilers, and later the Los Angeles Kings, he was NHL scoring champion and MVP nine times. In 1980, aged 19, he became the youngest player to be the season's top scorer. When he retired in 1999, he held records for career goals, points, and assists.

Who lost only one tennis match in 1983?

Martina Navratilova, the Czech player who became a U.S. citizen in 1981. She set new standards for women's tennis, winning 18 major singles titles and a world-record 167 singles tournaments.

What was the Chicago Bears' "one-man gang"?

This was how *Sports Illustrated* described Walter Payton. Between 1975 and 1987, the Bears' legendary runningback rushed for a record 16,726 yards, and broke O. J. Simpson's single-game record.

Who said: "You are the pits of the world!"

Hot-tempered genius John McEnroe, who won three Wimbledons and four US Opens, but in 1990 became the first player to be disqualified from a Grand Slam tournament for verbally abusing an umpire.

What did Reggie Jackson say about the World Series?

"The only reason I don't like playing in the World Series is I can't watch myself play." Jackson was called "Mr October" because of his outstanding record in World Series—which are played in that month.

One of the greatest-ever quarterbacks—Joe Montana.

Why did Carl Lewis wear red stilettos?

F OR A TIRE ADVERTISEMENT. LEWIS IS POSSIBLY THE ATHLETE OF the century, with nine Olympic golds. He won four golds, broke the 100 meters record at the 1984 Games, and won the long jump in four consecutive Olympics.

Which sisters-in-law won four golds at the 1988 Olympics?
Florence "Flo-Jo" Griffith-Joyner, famous for her multi-colored fingernails, won the gold in the 100 meters, 200 meters, and relay sprints. Her sister-in-law Jackie Joyner-Kersee won the gold in the heptathlon with a world-record 7,291 points.

How did Carl Lewis win Olympic gold by coming second?
In the 1988 Seoul Olympics in Korea, he was beaten in the 100 meters by Canadian Ben Johnson, who ran an astonishing 9.79 seconds. It was proved to be too astonishing—Johnson failed a drugs test and the gold went to Lewis.

Why did basketball star of the 80s "Magic" Johnson retire in 1991?
He had been infected with the HIV virus. Combining height, speed, and skill, Johnson had transformed the position of guard, winning five championships with the LA Lakers, and setting a record for assists.

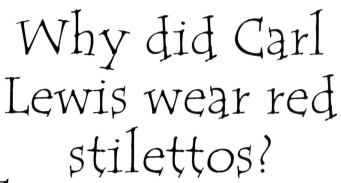

Carl Lewis stayed at the peak of condition for over ten years.

Which sporting hero defied gravity?

Basketball's greatest player, Michael Jordan, who became known as "His Airness" because he possessed an unbelievable ability to change direction in mid-air. He won six NBA Championships with the Chicago Bulls, and was MVP in every final. Jordan had the highest-ever scoring average, won two Olympic golds, earned the most money in sporting history ($300 million), and appeared on *Sports Illustrated*'s cover a record 42 times (beating Muhammad Ali's total of 34).

Which tennis star threw up on court?

"Pistol" Pete Sampras threw up on court during a fifth-set tiebreak against Alex Corretja, on his way to winning the U.S. Open in 1996. Sampras won Wimbledon six times in seven years, and has earned over $32 million in prize-money.

What happened to Nancy Kerrigan before the 1994 Winter Olympics?

THE ICE SKATER WAS ATTACKED AND struck on the knee to try to prevent her competing. Her arch-rival Tonya Harding was accused of being involved and was later sentenced to three years probation.

Nancy Kerrigan eventually won silver at the 1994 winter Olympics.

What happened in the 1997 Masters?

Tiger Woods takes a shot.

Tiger Woods became the youngest golfer to win the Masters, and the first black player to win a Major tournament. Woods had already won $1 million in only nine tournaments. He not only won the Masters, but hit a record 18 under par, and won by an astonishing 12 shots. The tournament is held in Augusta, whose founder Clifford Roberts once said, "As long as I'm alive, golfers will be white and caddies will be black."

What record did Mark McGwire shatter?

In 1998, McGwire broke the famous record for home runs in a season. He hit 70 homers for the St. Louis Cardinals to overtake both Babe Ruth and Roger Maris. The ball he hit for the last homer was sold for $2.7 million.

What did Greg Maddux and Pedro Martinez sign in 1997?

Maddux of the Atlanta Braves and Martinez of the Boston Red Sox each signed record contracts for $11.5 million a year. Maddux was the first player to win the Cy Young trophy for four consecutive years.

What did George Foreman win in 1994?

At the age of 45, the "punching preacher" became the oldest boxer to win a version of the world heavyweight title, by defeating Michael Moorer. He said, "I proved that 40 is no death sentence."

Who is Mia Hamm?

Probably the best female soccer player ever. She scored 103 goals between 1989 and 1994 as her university won four college championships and lost only one match. She played for the national team at the age of 15, and won the Women's World Cup at 19.

Who were the "dream team"?

Because of changes in the rules, professionals could compete in the 1992 Barcelona Olympics. The U.S. won the basketball gold by forming a "dream team" of sporting heroes including Michael Jordan and "Magic" Johnson.

Why was Mike Tyson fined a record $2,980,000?

He bit off part of Evander Holyfield's ear during their bout in 1997. Holyfield will be remembered as a dignified champion. Tyson, who became the youngest-ever heavyweight champ age 20 in 1986, will unfortunately be remembered for this incident and a three-year prison sentence for rape.

What happened to Jim Thorpe's Olympic medals in 1982?

The IOC finally admitted that it had been wrong, and returned Thorpe's gold medals to his family. Thorpe had died penniless in 1953. He was buried in Mauch Chunk, Pennsylvania, which changed its name to Jim Thorpe, and used his grave as a tourist attraction.

Why do no baseball players wear the number 42?

In 1997, Jackie Robinson's number was retired to celebrate the 50th anniversary of his breaking baseball's color barrier.

How did the great John L. Sullivan end his days?

Sullivan, who had been a very heavy drinker, ended up touring the country giving lectures on temperance.

Who lit the torch for the 1996 Atlanta Olympics?

Muhammad Ali, in a ceremony made more moving by his suffering from Parkinson's Syndrome. Ali became the first man to twice regain the heavyweight title when he defeated Leon Spinks in 1978. A later comeback against Larry Holmes in 1980, in which Ali retired after 10 rounds of punishment, contributed to this syndrome. In Atlanta, he moved slowly and his hands shook, but Ali retained extraordinary dignity.

Which sporting heroes have trophies names after them?

You know that you have become a sporting legend when a trophy gets named after you. The Cy Young Award is given to each season's best pitcher. An award for best college football player is named after Walter Payton.

What is the "House That Ruth Built"?

YANKEE STADIUM, BUILT IN 1923 WITH MONEY FROM THE AUDIENCES

Babe Ruth attracted. The Red Sox sold him to the New York Yankees for $125,000 in 1920. He led the Yankees four World Series, and christened the new stadium with a home run.

The Yankee Stadium is the home of baseball.

Why was Mildred Didrikson's last U.S. Open golf title so incredible?

She won by 12 strokes in 1954, only a year after having surgery for cancer. This remarkable sporting hero finally succumbed to the disease the following year.

Which sporting heroes went into showbusiness?

Many of them. Jack Johnson ended his days performing with a flea circus. Jesse Owens raced against horses to make a living. Jim Brown starred in the 1966 movie *The Dirty Dozen*.

O.J. Simpson was one of the sporting heroes of the seventies.

Which sporting hero faced a murder trial?

IN 1994, O. J. SIMPSON WAS ARRESTED, AFTER A TELEVISED POLICE CHASE, and charged with the brutal murder of his ex-wife Nicole Brown and her friend Ronald Goldman. Simpson had retired as a football player in 1979, and become a famous commentator and comic actor. His trial in 1995 was also televised and attracted huge publicity. In 1995, Simpson was controversially found not guilty.

Great Americans

Who is Uncle Sam?

Nobody. Uncle Sam is a nickname for the United States government. Nobody knows for certain the origin of the name, but it could have come from Samuel Wilson (1766—1854), an inspector of army supplies, who was nicknamed Uncle Sam.

Who was the greatest president?

In 1962, a group of historians made a list of presidents in order of greatness. Top of the list was Abraham Lincoln (1809—1865). Lincoln was president during the Civil War (1861—1865), when the northern states (the Unionists), who wanted slavery abolished, fought the southern states (the Confederates), who wanted to keep it. Lincoln was assassinated soon after the Unionists had won victory.

Apart from being a great scientist, Franklin organized the first volunteer fire brigade and founded the first free public library.

Which great statesman invented the lightning conductor?

Benjamin Franklin (1706—1790) signed the Declaration of Independence in 1776 as a representative of Pennsylvania. He also served as an ambassador to France, where he got French support for America's independence. Before his political career, Franklin worked as a scientist, mainly investigating electricity. He proved that lightning is caused by electricity and invented the lightning conductor.

Who signed the Declaration of Independence?

On July 4, 1776, 13 British colonies declared themselves independent of Britain and formed the United States of America. Representatives from each of the colonies signed a document, named the Declaration of Independence. Among them were Benjamin Franklin, Thomas Jefferson (1743—1826), and John Hancock (1737—93).

Which president won a Nobel Prize?

Woodrow Wilson (1856—1924), the 28th president of the United States. He was awarded the Nobel Prize for Peace in 1919 for his work in forming the League of Nations, the forerunner of the United Nations.

Which American was the first woman Member of Parliament in Britain?

Nancy Witcher Langhorne (1879—1964) was born in Virginia. In 1906 she married Waldorf Astor and moved to England. In 1919 Nancy Astor was elected Member of Parliament for Plymouth, southern England. She served in Parliament until 1945.

Which president was ambassador to Britain?

John Adams (1735—1826) was the first U.S. ambassador to Britain in 1785, two years after the United States' independence was recognized. Adams returned to the United States in 1788, to be elected vice president and then president (1797—1801).

Who was the first president of the United States?

George Washington (1732—1799), who was elected president in 1789. Washington led the Continental army against the British during the American Revolution. He served two terms in office.

In his first year as Secretary of State, Kissinger signed the cease-fire agreement ending the Vietnam War.

Which diplomat invented a shuttle?

Henry Kissinger (born 1923) was Secretary of State from 1973 to 1977. In 1974 he helped to arrange a cease-fire in the Arab-Israeli War by visiting and talking to each opposing side in turn. This became known as shuttle diplomacy.

Who helped to warm the Cold War?

WILLIAM A HARRIMAN (1891—1968) WAS A LONG-SERVING DIPLOMAT.

During World War II he was ambassador to the former Soviet Union, and in the 1960s he helped to negotiate the Nuclear Test-Ban Treaty.

Who gave his life to abolish slavery?

Abolitionists were people who wanted to end slavery in the United States. In 1859 John Brown (1800—1859) made a plan to free slaves in the southern states. With 21 comrades he captured an arsenal of weapons at Harpers Ferry, Virginia. He was captured by troops and hanged a few days later. He kept up his antislavery position during his trial.

Who were the suffragettes?

SUFFRAGETTES WERE PEOPLE WHO

campaigned for equal rights for women. One of the most famous suffragettes in the United States was Elizabeth Cady Stanton (1815—1902), who was head of the National Woman's Suffrage Association. Lucretia Mott and Susan Anthony were other famous suffragettes.

Elizabeth Stanton based her ideas on the Declaration of Independence.

Who was the first American saint?

Elizabeth Ann Seton (1774—1821) founded the Society for the Relief of Poor Widows with Small Children in 1797, and the Sisters of Charity in 1813. She was canonized (made a saint) in 1963.

Which famous novelist was on the side of the poor?

Upton Sinclair (1878—1968) was a novelist who was also a socialist. He wrote about the exploitation of poor immigrant workers in industry, and campaigned for reforms. He won the Pulitzer Prize in 1943.

Who was Jane Addams?

Jane Addams (1860—1935) was a social worker who fought against urban poverty in the United States. In 1889 she founded a famous community center in Chicago called Hull House. She shared the Nobel Prize for Peace in 1931.

Who is the world's most famous preacher?

Baptist minister Billy Graham (born 1918) is the world's most famous evangelist. He has been organizing preaching tours since 1944. On a tour in 1949 he preached to a total of 350,000 people in Los Angeles and two million people in Madison Square Gardens, New York City.

Who was an angel in battle?

The National Society of the Red Cross in the United States was founded in 1881 by Clara Barton (1821—1912). She was its president until 1904. As a nurse during the Civil War, Clara Barton was known as the "angel of the battlefield."

Who had a dream?

MARTIN LUTHER KING (1929—1968) WAS A Baptist clergyman and leader in the civil rights movement, which campaigned for equal rights for black Americans in the 1950s and 1960s. In 1963 he made a famous speech. "I have a dream," he said, "that my four little children will one day live in a nation where they will not be judged by the color of their skin, but by the content of their character." Martin Luther King was assassinated in Memphis, Tennessee, in 1968.

Who founded thousands of libraries?

Andrew Carnegie (1835—1919) was an industrialist who was born in Scotland and emigrated to the United States in 1848. He made a fortune in the steel business, which he used to build more than 2,800 public libraries worldwide.

Martin Luther King vowed to use "passive resistance and the weapon of love" to fight prejudice.

Who led the Apaches?

Cochise (1815—1874) led his Apache warriors

against the U.S. army in Arizona during the 1860s, after soldiers had killed his relatives. Cochise finally surrendered in 1871.

Who led the Union in the Civil War?

The two main men were Ulysses S. Grant (1822—1885) and William Tecumseh Sherman (1820—1891). Grant won several battles before becoming commander-in-chief of all U.S. armies in 1864. Sherman was commander of U.S. forces in the western area.

Cochise's revenge for the deaths of his relatives was so effective that troops, settlers and traders all left the region.

Who was Paul Revere?

Paul Revere (1735—1818) was a folk hero of the American Revolution, during which the United States won its independence from Britain. After a career as a silversmith in Boston, Revere became a courier for the rebels. In 1775 he rode from Boston to Lexington to warn revolutionary leaders that British troops were on the way. This journey was made famous in a poem by Henry Longfellow called *Paul Revere's Ride*.

Who led the Confederates?

Thomas Jonathan Jackson (1824—1863) and Robert E. Lee (1807—1870). "Stonewall" Jackson was a brigadier general in the Confederate army. He was accidentally shot dead by one of his own men. General Lee commanded the army of Northern Virginia.

Who said: "Damn the torpedoes"?

David Glasgow Farragut (1801—1870) was a naval officer on the Union side in the Civil War. In 1864 his ships sailed to capture enemy forts in Mobile Bay, Alabama, which was protected by mines (called torpedoes at the time). Farragut sailed through the mines, crying: "Damn the torpedoes!"

Which racing driver became an air ace?

By 1914 Eddie Rickenbacker (1890—1973) was one of the top racing drivers in the United States. He then joined the army, became an army pilot, and shot down 26 enemy planes during World War I. He eventually became president of Eastern Air Lines.

Who is the U.S.S. *Nimitz* named after?

U.S.S. *Nimitz* is one of the largest aircraft carriers in the world. It is named after Admiral Chester William Nimitz (1885—1966). Nimitz served in submarines in World War I and was commander of U.S. naval forces in the Pacific in World War II.

Which naval hero was killed in a duel?

Stephen Decatur (1779—1820) was the naval officer who led a raid on Tripoli harbor, in Libya, in 1804 to destroy a captured U.S. ship. He was awarded the sword of honor. Decatur was killed in a duel with a fellow officer.

Eisenhower became president in 1953 and remained in power for eight years.

Who led the U.S. in World War II?

DWIGHT D. EISENHOWER (1890—1969) JOINED THE ARMY DURING WORLD War I and served until 1948. In 1943, during World War II, he became a general and was given the title of Supreme Allied Commander. He was ordered to plan the Allied invasion of Europe, Operation Overlord, which began with the D-day la·dings in France on June 6, 1944.

The Model-T was known as "the motor car for the multitude."

Who got rich with sleeping?

IN 1859 GEORGE MORTIMER PULLMAN (1831—1897) STARTED UP A BUSINESS converting regular railroad cars into luxury sleeping cars. His Pullman Palace Car Company made him a fortune, with which he built a town, now part of Chicago. "Pullman" is now used to describe any luxury railroad carriage.

Who started an industry with a Model-T?
The Model-T was the first mass-produced car. It was made by the Ford Motor Company, which was started in 1903 by Henry Ford (1863—1947). More than 15 million Model-Ts were made and sold.

Who got rich by keeping warm?
John Jacob Astor (1763—1848) was born in Germany and emigrated to the United States with no money. He started with a small shop in New York City selling furs and built up the American Fur Company. He became the richest man in the U.S.

Who got rich by staying cold?
Clarence Birdseye (1886—1956) was an inventor who started the frozen food industry. One of his experiments was to try to keep food fresh for long periods by freezing it. The freezing process he developed kept the flavor of the food while it was frozen.

Who made a fortune from software?
Bill Gates (born 1955) is the man that founded Microsoft, the company which created the operating systems MS-DOS and Windows. These programs are now used on almost every PC in the world. Gates left university early to start Microsoft with a friend, and became a billionaire in 1986 when the company was floated on the stock market.

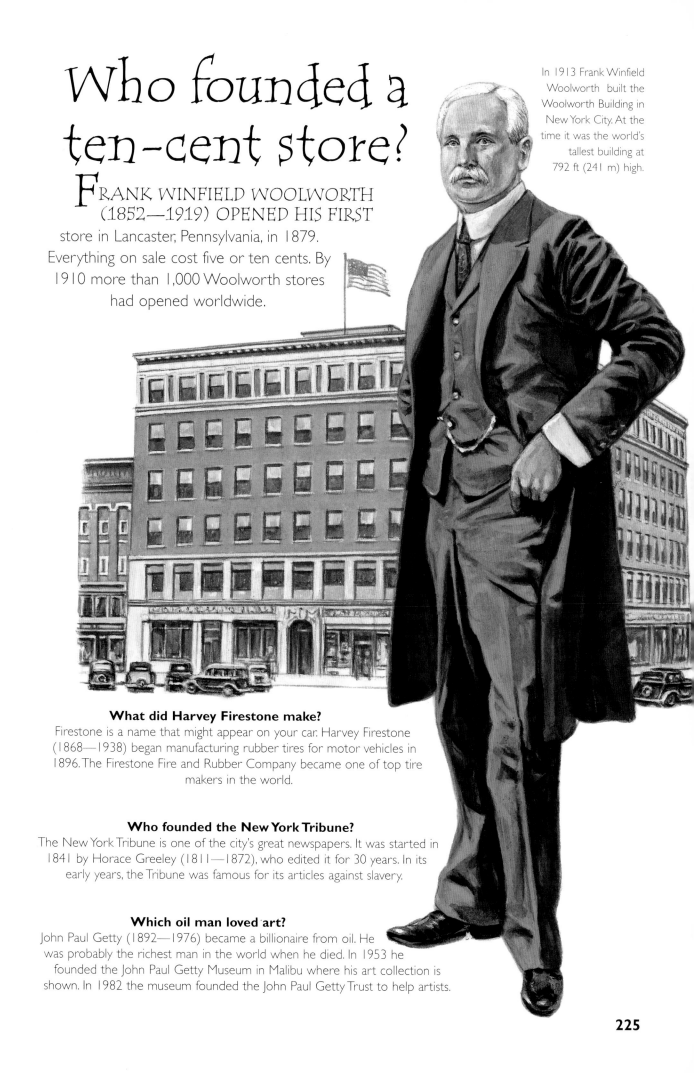

Who founded a ten-cent store?

FRANK WINFIELD WOOLWORTH (1852—1919) OPENED HIS FIRST store in Lancaster, Pennsylvania, in 1879. Everything on sale cost five or ten cents. By 1910 more than 1,000 Woolworth stores had opened worldwide.

In 1913 Frank Winfield Woolworth built the Woolworth Building in New York City. At the time it was the world's tallest building at 792 ft (241 m) high.

What did Harvey Firestone make?
Firestone is a name that might appear on your car. Harvey Firestone (1868—1938) began manufacturing rubber tires for motor vehicles in 1896. The Firestone Fire and Rubber Company became one of top tire makers in the world.

Who founded the New York Tribune?
The New York Tribune is one of the city's great newspapers. It was started in 1841 by Horace Greeley (1811—1872), who edited it for 30 years. In its early years, the Tribune was famous for its articles against slavery.

Which oil man loved art?
John Paul Getty (1892—1976) became a billionaire from oil. He was probably the richest man in the world when he died. In 1953 he founded the John Paul Getty Museum in Malibu where his art collection is shown. In 1982 the museum founded the John Paul Getty Trust to help artists.

Who disappeared while flying around the world?

AMELIA EARHART (1897—1937) WAS A PIONEERING AVIATOR. IN 1932 she became the first woman to fly nonstop across the Atlantic Ocean solo and to fly nonstop from coast to coast across the United States. In 1937 she attempted to fly around the world with copilot Frederick Noonan. Their aircraft disappeared after leaving New Guinea. It was never found.

Amelia's plane is thought to have gone down off the coast of Howland Island, near Honolulu.

Who was the first person to find the North Pole?

Robert Edwin Peary (1856—1920) was an explorer who made several expeditions to the Arctic around the turn of the century. On April 6, 1909, he became first person to reach the North Pole.

Who flew around the world alone?

Wiley Post (1899—1935) was a pilot who set many aviation records. In 1933 he flew around the world solo in a Lockheed Vega aircraft in just under eight days. Post was killed in a plane crash.

Who made the first solo flight over the Atlantic Ocean?

Charles Lindburgh (1902—1974) made his flight in his aircraft *Spirit of St Louis* on May 20—21, 1927. The flight between New York and Paris, France took 33 hours and 39 minutes. Lindburgh's main problem was staying awake.

Who was the first American to fly around the Earth in space?

Lieutenant Colonel John Glenn made three orbits of the Earth in a Friendship capsule launched by a Mercury rocket on February 20, 1962. The flight lasted nearly five hours.

Which around-the-world sailor could not swim?

Joshua Slocum (1844—1910) spent most of his life at sea. In 1898, after retiring as a ship's captain, he set out in an old fishing boat named *Spray* to become the first yachtsman to sail around the world solo. But Slocum could not swim and disappeared at sea with *Spray* in 1910.

Who led an expedition to the West?

The Lewis and Clark expedition set out in 1804 to explore overland to the Pacific coast of America. In charge was Captain Meriwether Lewis (1774—1809). The explorers returned two and half years later having covered 8,000 miles (13,000 km).

Who helped found the American Geographical Society?

Adolphus Washington Greely (1844—1935). From 1881 to 1883 Greely carried out an exploration of Greenland that ended in tragedy when all but six of his 25 men died of hunger during the winter.

Which bird flew over the North Pole in 1924?

Richard Evelyn Byrd (1888—1957) was a naval flier and explorer. In 1926 he became the first person to fly over the North Pole. Byrd also made five expeditions to the Antarctic and set up a U.S. Antarctic base.

When Apollo 11 landed on the Moon the astronauts said "The Eagle has landed."

Who made a giant leap for mankind?

ON JULY 21, 1969, THE LUNAR MODULE OF APOLLO 11 landed on the Moon. Its commander Neil Alden Armstrong (born 1930) was the first man to step onto the Moon's surface, saying: "This is one small step for man, one giant leap for mankind." His fellow astronaut Buzz Aldrin followed him down the ladder.

Disney's first theme park, Disneyland, opened in California in 1955.

Which actress has won the most Oscars?

Katherine Hepburn (born 1907) has won most Oscars in the Best Actress category, with four from 13 nominations. She was awarded her first for *Morning Glory* (1933) and her last for *On Golden Pond* (1981) when she was 74.

Which man with a girl's name played tough cowboys?

Marion Michael Morrison, better known as John Wayne (1906—1979), and often called simply "Duke," was famous for playing tough cowboys and soldiers in westerns and war films. He appeared in more than 150 feature films. His first major role was as the Ringo Kid in *Stagecoach* in 1939. He was presented with an Academy Award in 1969 for the part of Rooster Cogburn in *True Grit*.

Who are the great American film directors?

A difficult question! Everybody will have their favorite. Some of the big names to look up are Frank Capra (1897—1991), Howard Hawks (1896—1977), John Ford (1895—1973), Stanley Kubrick (1928—1999), Francis Ford Coppola (born 1939), George Lucas (born 1945), and Steven Spielberg (born 1946).

What sort of show did Barnum run?

A circus. Phineas Taylor Barnum (1810—1891) was a showman who opened his own circus in 1871. Modestly, he named it "The Greatest Show on Earth." In 1881 he joined forces with a rival to form the famous Barnum and Bailey Circus.

Who invented a cartoon mouse?

THE MAN WHO STARTED DISNEY FILMS, WALTER ELIAS (WALT) DISNEY (1901—1966). In 1928 Walt Disney invented the character Mickey Mouse and made the first Mickey Mouse movie, *Steamboat Willie*. Disney released *Snow White and the Seven Dwarfs*, the first feature-length animated movie, in 1938.

Who was Buffalo Bill?

BUFFALO BILL'S REAL NAME WAS WILLIAM

Frederick Cody (1846—1917). He was a scout for the U.S. army and a buffalo hunter. In 1883 he started Buffalo Bill's Wild West Show, which toured towns and cities across the U.S., with exhibitions of hunting, riding, and shooting.

Who are America's greatest actors?

Pick from Marlon Brando (born 1924), Humphrey Bogart (1899 —1957), Henry Fonda (1905—1982), John Wayne (1907—1979), Katherine Hepburn (born 1907), Bette Davis (1908—1989), James Stewart (1908—1997), Jane Fonda (born 1937), Dustin Hoffman (born 1937), Robert de Niro (born 1943), Meryl Streep (born 1949), Tom Hanks (born 1956), or Michelle Pfeiffer (born 1957). Or choose your own!

Which newscaster was the face of CBS?

Walter Cronkite (born 1916) came to fame as a CBS newscaster. Between 1962 and 1981 he was anchorman of the CBS evening news program. His face became known in every U.S. home.

Which magician escaped from everything?

Harry Houdini (1874—1926), real name Erich Weiss. Houdini became world famous as a magician and escapologist. His trademark trick was to escape from a sealed container full of water after being handcuffed and put in a straitjacket.

Who is America's most popular talk show host?

Oprah Winfrey (born 1954), who is known to most viewers simply as Oprah. She began her career as a news presenter for CBS at 19. The Oprah Winfrey Show started in 1986.

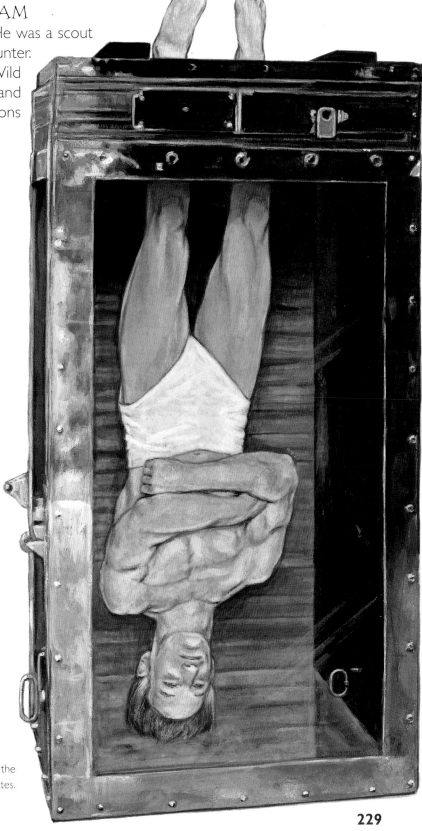

Houdini was born in Hungary but lived in the United States.

What did Ernest Hemingway write about?

Ernest Hemingway (1889—1961) was one of the greatest American writers. He wrote novels—about brave people living dangerous lives, especially during wars—such as *A Farewell to Arms* (1929) and *For Whom the Bell Tolls* (1940).

Hemingway's novel *The Old Man and the Sea* won him the Nobel prize for literature in 1954.

Who went with the wind?

Margaret Mitchell (1900—1949) wrote only one novel, and it took her 10 years to complete. But it became one of the most famous novels of all time. It was *Gone with the Wind*, a story about a family in Georgia during and after the Civil War. It was published in 1936 and became an instant bestseller. It was made into an even more famous film of the same name in 1939.

Who wrote Little Women?

LOUISA MAY ALCOTT (1832—1888) WAS A NURSE DURING THE CIVIL WAR. SHE completed her most famous book, *Little Women*, in 1869. It is about life in an American family during the 1800s.

Who wrote *Uncle Tom's Cabin*?

Uncle Tom's Cabin was the first antislavery novel to be published in the United States. It was written in 1852 by Harriet Beecher Stowe (1811—1896) and became a very popular book and play. It helped the antislavery cause before the Civil War.

Who are the greatest poets of the U.S?

Difficult to say! Two of the best are Walt Whitman (1819—1892) and Henry Wadsworth Longfellow (1807—1882). Whitman was a Civil War nurse and wrote war poetry. Longfellow was a popular poet who wrote *Paul Revere's Ride*.

230

Who was Huckleberry Finn?

H UCKLEBERRY FINN WAS A FICTIONAL
CHARACTER IN THE BOOK THE
Adventures of Huckleberry Finn, published in 1884. It was
written by Mark Twain (1835—1910), one of the greatest
writers in the U.S. Twain's real name was Samuel Longhorn
Clemens. Before becoming a writer, Twain worked as a boat
pilot on the Mississippi River. His other famous novels
include *The Prince and the Pauper* (1882) and *The Adventures
of Tom Sawyer* (1876).

Which writer campaigned for civil rights?

James Baldwin (1924—1987) was a black American who wrote books, shorts stories, and plays about black Americans and race relations in the United States. In the 1950s he campaigned for civil rights for blacks.

Who was the first writer from the United States to win a Nobel Prize?

In 1930 Sinclair Lewis (1885—1951) became the first American to win a Nobel Prize for Literature. He wrote novels about the lives of middle-class Americans.

Whose most famous book is *The Grapes of Wrath*?

It was written in 1939 by John Steinbeck (1902—1968). It is a story about poor farmers living through a terrible drought in the 1930s.. Steinbeck won the Nobel Prize for Literature in 1962.

Whose first success was *The Glass Menagerie*?

The Glass Menagerie was written in 1944 by playwright Tennessee Williams (1914—1983). Williams wrote about the difficulties of life. Another famous play of his, *A Streetcar Named Desire*, won him a Pulitzer Prize.

Marlon Brando played the lead role in a film version of *A Streetcar Named Desire*.

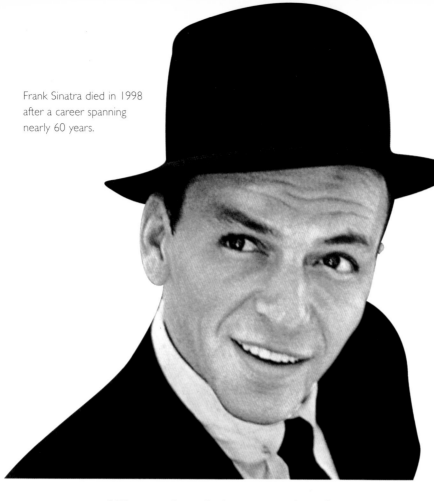

Frank Sinatra died in 1998 after a career spanning nearly 60 years.

Which singer was the King?

"The King" was the nickname of the great rock and roll singer Elvis Presley (1935—1977). He was also known as "Elvis the Pelvis" because of the way he moved his hips while he sang. As a teenager, Presley lived in Memphis, where he listened to rhythm and blues music. He came to fame in the mid-1950s with a new style of rock and roll music. He made 45 records, which sold more than a million copies. He also appeared in 33 films.

Which brothers wrote Broadway musicals?

George Gershwin (1898—1937) and Ira Gershwin (1896—1983) teamed up to write several Broadway musicals, including *Porgy and Bess*. George composed the musical scores and Ira wrote the lyrics.

Who was America's greatest singer?

Most people would say Frank Sinatra. He started his singing career in the mid-1930s and was world famous by the early 1940s, when he also started acting. He won an Oscar in 1953 for his role in *From Here to Eternity*.

Which rock and roll singer died aged 22?

Buddy Holly (1936—1959), whose real name was Charles Harden Holly. He was a singer, songwriter, and guitarist, who made several hit records with his group The Crickets in the 1950s. He was killed in a plane crash.

Who wrote "God Bless America"?

RUSSIAN-BORN SONGWRITER ISRAEL BALINE (1888—1989) MOVED TO the United States as a boy. When his first song was published, the printer had spelt his name Irving Berlin, so he named himself that. Irving Berlin became perhaps the greatest songwriter in the United States. He wrote nearly 800 songs, including *God Bless America*, and dozens of Broadway shows, including *Annie Get Your Gun*.

Who composed military marches?

John Philip Sousa (1854—1932). Between 1880 and 1892 Sousa was leader of the band of the U.S. Marines. He wrote more than 100 tunes for military marches, including *The Stars and Stripes Forever*.

Who invented the Jets and the Sharks?

The Jets and the Sharks were two gangs of youths in the musical *West Side Story*. It was one of the musicals written by Leonard Bernstein (1918—1990), a conductor and composer.

Which jazz player was a "Count"?

"Count" Basie (1904—1984) was not a real count. His proper name was William Basie. His nickname was thought up by a radio station presenter. Basie was a top jazz pianist and band leader.

Madonna is now the most photographed woman in the world.

Is Madonna the star's real name?

Yes, her full name is Madonna Louise Ciccone and she grew up in Pontiac, Michigan, a suburb of Detroit. Her father immigrated from Italy and her mother is French Canadian.

Who was Satchmo?

The jazz singer and trumpet player Louis Armstrong (1900—1971). Armstrong began singing in New Orleans as a teenager and became probably the most influential jazz musician of all time.

Frank Lloyd Wright was one of the most important figures in Western architecture.

Who designed a mile-high skyscraper?

FRANK LLOYD WRIGHT (1869—1959) WAS A FAMOUS AMERICAN ARCHITECT

who created extraordinary new styles of architecture. One of his most famous designs is the Guggenheim Museum in New York. Wright also designed many buildings that were never built, including a "mile-high" skyscraper, which would have been three times higher than the highest modern skyscrapers.

Which artist painted in London ... at night?
James Whistler (1834—1903) spent most of his working life outside the United States. He moved to Paris, France in 1855 and to London in 1859. During the 1870s he painted several famous pictures of London, England at night.

Who is famous for dripping paint?
Jackson Pollock (1912—1956) painted abstract pictures that revealed his feelings on the canvas instead of showing scenes of the real world. He often used the technique of dripping swirling lines of paint on to a huge canvas, which he called "action painting."

What did Buckminster Fuller invent?
Buckminster Fuller (1895—1983) was an architect and engineer who came up with several new ideas for building shapes. One of these was called the geodesic dome, which is a domed building made of a framework of triangles.

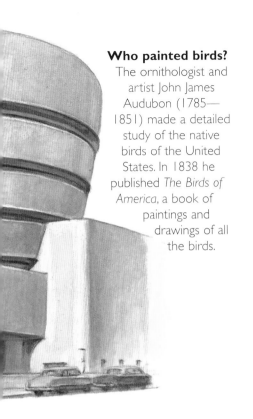

Who painted birds?

The ornithologist and artist John James Audubon (1785—1851) made a detailed study of the native birds of the United States. In 1838 he published *The Birds of America*, a book of paintings and drawings of all the birds.

Who was the first great portrait painter of the United States?

John Singleton Copley (1738—1815) was the greatest portrait painter of his time. He worked in Boston, New York City, Philadelphia, and London, England. His portraits included those of revolutionary hero Paul Revere and politician Samuel Adams.

Who is famous for sculpting people?

Poor eyesight prevented Sir Jacob Epstein (1880—1959) from being a painter. Instead he turned to sculpting, and became brilliant at creating figures of people. Epstein was born in New York City, and set up a studio in London, England, in 1905.

Who painted soup cans?

What did Ansel Adams do?

Ansel Adams (1902—1984) was a photographer. He took superb black-and-white photographs of landscapes, especially of the southwest of the United States. He also wrote many books on photographic technique.

THE ARTIST ANDY WARHOL (1928—1987). HE WAS ONE OF THE LEADERS OF A group of artists who started a new style of art called "pop art" in the early 1960s. The artists used everyday objects to make up their pictures. Warhol's most famous paintings are made up of lots of images of the same object, such as soup cans, in strange colors.

Andy Warhol was not just an artist, he was also involved in film-making, photography, and publishing.

From the age of 12, Einstein was determined to solve "the riddle of the world."

Who worked out that $E=mc^2$?

A man with one of the greatest scientific minds of all time, Albert Einstein (1879—1955). Einstein was a theoretical physicist. He was born in Germany, moved to the United States in 1940, and became an American citizen. His most famous works are his Special Theory of Relativity (1905) and General Theory of Relativity (1916). Part of the special theory stated that mass (m) can be changed into energy (E) according to the equation $E=mc^2$.

Who encouraged education?

Two of America's leading educationalists were Nicholas Murray Butler (1862—1947), who shared the Nobel Prize for Peace in 1931, and John Dewey (1859—1952), who lectured all over the world on education.

Whose name appears on every library book?

Melvil Dewey (1851—1931) was a famous librarian. He invented a system of classifying books by their subject named Dewey decimal. All library books have a Dewey number.

Who started a detective agency?

ALLAN PINKERTON (1819—1884) WAS IN CHARGE OF ARMY SPIES ON THE Union side during the Civil War. In 1850 he started a private detective agency in Chicago, which became the famous Pinkerton National Detective Agency.

Which mathematician took polls?

GEORGE HORACE GALLUP (1901—1984)
WAS A STATISTICIAN WHO
developed the Gallup Poll for judging public opinion on
subjects. The poll is taken by asking a random selection of
people simple questions.

What did Noah Webster write?
Books on the English language,
including spelling and grammar. Noah
Webster (1758—1843) was a
lexicographer (a writer of
dictionaries). In 1812 he
completed *The American Dictionary
of English Language*.

Bobby Fischer had an incredibly high
I.Q. He was the youngest grandmaster
in the history of chess, at 15.

Who are America's famous economists?
Milton Friedman (born 1912) and John Kenneth Galbraith
(born 1908). Friedman was professor at the University of
Chicago and won the 1976 Nobel Prize for Economics.
Galbraith taught at Harvard and was U.S. ambassador to
India in the 1960s.

Who was famous for checkmates?
The chess player Bobby Fischer (born 1943). Fischer
started playing when he was six and won the
American Championship at 15. In 1972 he won the
World Championship in one of the most famous
chess matches of all time. His opponent was Soviet
player Boris Spassky. The match took place during the
Cold War, and was seen as a battle between capitalism
and communism.

Who has a telescope named after him?

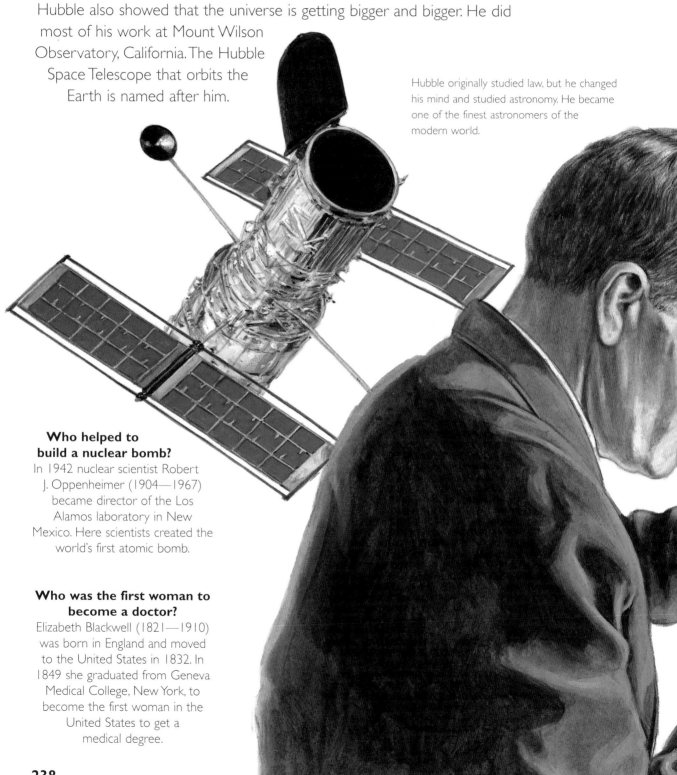

EDWIN POWELL HUBBLE (1889—1953), THE FAMOUS astronomer who was the first person to show that the universe is made up of huge groups of stars called galaxies with space between them. Hubble also showed that the universe is getting bigger and bigger. He did most of his work at Mount Wilson Observatory, California. The Hubble Space Telescope that orbits the Earth is named after him.

Hubble originally studied law, but he changed his mind and studied astronomy. He became one of the finest astronomers of the modern world.

Who helped to build a nuclear bomb?

In 1942 nuclear scientist Robert J. Oppenheimer (1904—1967) became director of the Los Alamos laboratory in New Mexico. Here scientists created the world's first atomic bomb.

Who was the first woman to become a doctor?

Elizabeth Blackwell (1821—1910) was born in England and moved to the United States in 1832. In 1849 she graduated from Geneva Medical College, New York, to become the first woman in the United States to get a medical degree.

What did Albert Michelson measure?

The speed of light. Albert Michelson (1852—1931) was a physicist who built a device called an interferometer, which he used to measure the speed of light far more accurately than it had been measured before. In 1907 he received the Nobel Prize for Physics.

Who discovered Barnard's Star?

No surprise here! It was the astronomer Edward Emerson Barnard (1857—1923). In 1916 Barnard discovered a star that is moving very quickly compared to the other stars. It is now called Barnard's star. Barnard also discovered 16 comets and a moon of Jupiter.

Who was a famous brain surgeon?

Harvey Williams Cushing (1869—1939). He was the first person to describe the medical syndrome (abnormality) that is now called Cushing's syndrome.

Pauling was the man who found the cause of the disease, sickle cell anaemia.

Who is the only man to win two Nobel prizes?

Linus Carl Pauling (1901—1994) was a brilliant chemist. He was awarded his first Nobel Prize (for chemistry) in 1954. In 1962 Pauling was awarded the Nobel Prize for Peace for his campaign against nuclear weapons testing.

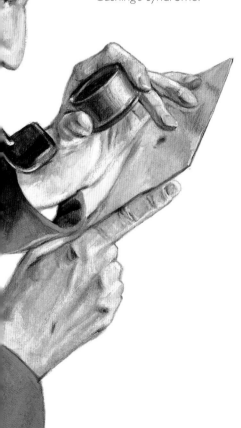

Who modeled DNA?

DNA IS A CHEMICAL THAT HOLDS THE CODE FOR HOW ALL ANIMALS and plants grow and live. The way the chemical's atoms are joined together was first modeled in 1953 by biologists James Dewey Watson (born 1928) from the United States and Francis Crick (born 1916) from Britain.

Who made rubber useful?

A process named vulcanization makes rubber last longer and makes it stay rubbery when it is very hot or very cold. The process was invented by Charles Goodyear (1800—1860) in 1839, and it allowed long-lasting vehicle tires to be made.

Who got the sewing machine going?

Isaac Merritt Singer (1811—1875). He marketed the first sewing machine for home use, which was patented in 1851. The Singer became a worldwide best seller. The sewing machine was actually invented in France in 1829 by Barthélemy Thimmonier.

Who invented a famous code?

Samuel Finley Breese Morse (1791—1872) was an inventor and a pioneer of the electric telegraph—a device for sending messages along wires. Morse invented a code of dots and dashes that represent letters and numbers. It is known as Morse code.

What did Chester Floyd Carlson copy?

Anything written on paper—he invented xerography (now called photocopying) in 1938. Chester Floyd Carlson (1906—1968) founded a company that is now the Xerox Corporation.

Who said: "Come in here, Watson"?

THE INVENTOR OF THE TELEPHONE,

Alexander Graham Bell (1847—1922). Bell was born in Scotland. He was interested in speech therapy, and taught people with hearing difficulties how to speak at a school in Boston. In 1876 he demonstrated an invention that allowed speech to be sent along a wire—the telephone. His first words on his telephone were: "Come in here, Watson," spoken to his assistant, who was in the next room.

The first name for the telephone was the "electric speech machine."

Edison founded the Edison Electric Light Company in 1878.

Which brothers built the first airplane?

The Wright brothers — Orville (1871—1948) and Wilbur (1867—1912). In December 1903, at Kitty Hawk, North Carolina, their home-built plane *Flyer* made the first proper controlled flight by a powered aircraft.

How did Robert Hutchings Goddard rocket to fame?

He was a builder of rockets. In 1926 Robert Hutchings Goddard (1882—1945) developed the first rocket fueled by liquids rather than solid fuel.

Who made elevators safe?

In 1852 Elisha Graves Otis (1811—1861) invented a safety device that stopped goods elevators falling to the ground if the rope broke. This allowed safe passenger elevators to be developed.

Which telegraph operator invented light bulbs?

Thomas Alva Edison (1847—1931) was probably the greatest inventor of all. He worked as telegraph operator on the American railroads during the 1860s, where he got the idea for a new type of telegraph machine. He also invented a light bulb, the microphone and the phonograph, which was the forerunner of the record player.

Who helped us to take holiday snaps?

GEORGE EASTMAN (1854—1932) WAS A PIONEER OF PHOTOGRAPHY. IN 1888 he developed the first simple camera that was sold to the public, the Kodak camera. It was loaded with film that the owner could send off for processing.

Which great tennis player became a citizen of the United States?

Martina Navratilova was born in 1956 in Czechoslovakia, and by the age of 17 she had been national champion three times. She became a U.S. citizen in 1981, and then won 18 Grand Slam singles titles, including a record nine at Wimbledon, England.

Who started life as Cassius Clay?

The heavyweight boxer Muhammad Ali (born 1942). He was born as Cassius Clay, and changed his name in 1964 after becoming a Muslim. Ali was the only boxer to win the heavyweight world championship three times, in 1964, 1974, and 1978. He won 56 of his 61 professional fights. Ali proclaimed himself as *The Greatest*, and made up raplike poems about himself.

Peter Sampras is rated the number one tennis player in the world.

Who ran to fame in 1936?

The sprinter Jesse Owens (1913—1980). Owens' real name was James Cleveland, and his initials JC were turned into Jesse by his school teacher. At 22, he set four world sprinting and jumping records in the space of 45 minutes. At the 1936 Olympics in Berlin, Owens won four gold medals — the 100 meters, the 200 meters, the long jump, and the sprint relay.

Which tennis tournament has Pete Sampras not won?

DESPITE HIS GREAT CAREER SUCCESS, SAMPRAS HAS NEVER GOT further than the semifinals in the French Open. The games are played on red clay courts and Sampras does not enjoy playing on them and sees the Open as a major challenge.

Who was the greatest all-around athlete?

At the 1912 Stockholm Olympics, Sweden, where Jim Thorpe (1888—1953) won both the pentathlon and decathlon, the King of Sweden said to him: "Sir, you are the greatest athlete in the world." Thorpe also played professional baseball and football.

Who was named Golfer of the Century?

IN 1988 THE PROFESSIONAL GOLF ASSOCIATION OF THE United States named Jack Nicklaus (born 1940) Golfer of the Century. He became a professional golfer in 1961, and a year later became youngest player to win the U.S. Open, the first of his 20 championship wins.

Who is the greatest quarterback?

Joe Montana (born 1956) dominated the National Football League during the 1980s playing for the San Francisco 49ers. With Montana in command, they won the Super Bowl four times, three times with Montana as Most Valuable Player.

Who swam to seven Olympic golds?

At the 1972 Olympics in Munich, U.S. swimmer Mark Spitz (born 1950) made history by winning seven gold medals, four in individual events and three in relays.

What is The House that Ruth Built?

Yankee Stadium, home of the New York Yankees baseball team. It got its nickname from Babe Ruth (1895—1948), the greatest baseball batter of all time, who played in it throughout the 1920s. He hit a record 714 home runs in his career.

Who is "Magic" on a basketball court?

The basketball player Earvin "Magic" Johnson (born 1959). For the Los Angeles Lakers, Johnson was Most Valuable Player, three times as the Lakers won five NBA titles. He played in the U.S. Dream Team at the 1992 Olympics, despite being diagnosed HIV positive in 1991.

What did the Kennedy brothers do?

There were three brothers in the most famous political family in the United States. Their father was Joseph Patrick Kennedy (1888—1969). John Fitzgerald Kennedy (1917—1963) was inaugurated as president in 1961, and assassinated in 1963. Robert Francis Kennedy (1925—1968) was attorney general, and was assassinated in 1968 while running for president. Edward Moore Kennedy (born 1932) is a senator.

Who were the Rockefellers?

The Rockefellers are a family of entrepreneurs. John Davison Rockefeller (1839—1937) made a huge fortune in oil refining. His son John D. Rockefeller (1874—1960), built the Rockefeller Center in New York City, and his son, Nelson Rockefeller (1908—1970), was vice president from 1974 to 1977.

How did Laurel meet Hardy?

Stan Laurel (1890—1965) and Oliver Hardy (1892—1957) were a comedy duo who made nearly 90 slapstick films. The two men joined a film studio separately in 1926, and the studio owner persuaded them to team up.

What did Rodgers and Hammerstein write?

Oscar Hammerstein (1895—1960) wrote the lyrics to many musicals, and often teamed up with the composer Richard Rodgers (1902—1979). Together they created famous musicals such as *Oklahoma!* and *The King and I*.

Who founded their own museum?

THE GUGGENHEIMS ARE A FAMILY OF INDUSTRIALISTS. MEYER Guggenheim (1828—1905) emigrated from Switzerland in 1847 and had seven sons. One of the seven, Simon Guggenheim (1861—1949) started a foundation that helped artists and writers. Another, Solomon Robert Guggenheim, started a foundation that built the famous Guggenheim Museum in New York City.

Who were the Jackson Five?

A SINGING GROUP, MADE UP OF FIVE SONS OF the Jackson family. They made records on the famous Motown label. The most famous member of the group is Michael, who was just 8 when the group formed.

What were the names of the Marx brothers?
The Marx brothers were a zany comedy team who performed on stage and in films, such as *A Night at the Opera*. The main members of the team were Groucho (1895—1977), Harpo (1893—1964), and Chico (1891—1961).

How were the two President Roosevelts related?
Theodore Roosevelt (1858—1919), the 26th president, was a fifth cousin of Franklin D. Roosevelt (1882—1945), the 32nd president.

What did the Maxim family make?
Guns and ammunition. Sir Hiram Stevens Maxim (1840—1916) invented the Maxim machine gun, which was the first fully automatic machine gun. His brother Hudson Maxim (1853—1927) developed high explosives, and his son Hiram Percy Maxim (1869—1936) invented the silencer.

The first Jackson Five single in 1970 was *I Want You Back*. It sold two million copies.

Quiz questions

THE 50 STATES

1. In which state is **Crater Lake National Park**?

2. What is one of **Montana's** nicknames?

3. Where did **Custer's Last Stand** take place?

4. Which cartoon character did **George Shultz** create?

5. What was **John Wayne's** real name?

6. What is **Methuselah**?

7. Which strange monster can you meet in **Arizona**?

8. Who did the Texans fight at the **Alamo**?

9. Which state is famous for its red chickens?

10. What did **John Brown** campaign for?

11. Which "king" lived in **Memphis**?

12. Which is the only state to produce diamonds?

13. What does "**Mardi Gras**" mean?

PILGRIMS

1. Who lived in longhouses?

2. Who drew Native American scenes?

3. Who did John Rolfe marry?

4. Which country in Europe did the pilgrims first leave?

5. What is the name of the ship that carried the Pilgrim Fathers to America?

6. Who was the chief of the Morattigan?

7. When was the first Thanksgiving?

8. Who was Maryland named after?

9. Who founded Quebec?

10. What was King Philip's real name?

11. What happened on July 4, 1776?

NATIVE AMERICANS

1. What did Benjamin Franklin base the American constitution on?

2. What does "Sioux" mean?

3. What game originated from a game played by the Choctaw?

4. What does Nez Perce mean?

5. What were eagle feathers used for?

6. What were porcupine hairs and sticks used for?

7. What are moccasins?

8. What was the name of a Hopi trial marriage?

9. Which dance was said to restore old traditions?

10. How did some Native Americans try to get rid of their troubles?

Quiz answers

THE 50 STATES
1. Oregon.
2. Big Sky Country
3. Dakota
4. Peanuts
5. Marion Morrison
6. A giant bristlecone pine tree
7. Gila monster
8. The Mexicans
9. Rhode Island
10. The abolition of slavery
11. Elvis Presley
12. Arkansas
13. Fat Tuesday

PILGRIMS
1. The Iroquois
2. John White
3. Pocohontas
4. The Netherlands
5. The *Mayflower*
6. Samoset
7. 1621
8. The Virgin Mary
9. Champlain
10. Metacomet
11. The Declaration of Independence

NATIVE AMERICANS
1. The Iroquois Confederacy
2. Enemy
3. Lacrosse
4. Pierced nose
5. Currency
6. Brushing teeth
7. Shoes
8. *Dumaiya*
9. The Ghost Dance
10. By burning the Cry Shed down

HOW THE WEST WAS WON
1. Tepee
2. Shells
3. Gold
4. Jefferson
5. They were fur trappers
6. The Mormons
7. Cholera
8. President Polk
9. Levi Strauss
10. A railroad that linked the East and West.
11. To pump water

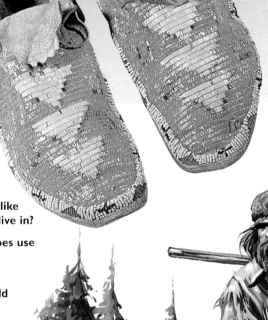

HOW THE WEST WAS WON

1. What is the name for the tentlike homes some Native Americans live in?

2. What did the Pacific coast tribes use instead of money?

3. What did the Spanish Conquistadors believe they would find in the Americas?

4. Who sent Jefferson and Clark on an expedition?

5. What did mountain men do?

6. Which church was Brigham Young the head of?

7. Which disease caused many deaths during the Oregon and California trails?

8. Which president had to prove to his government that there was gold in the hills?

9. Who invented jeans?

10. What did the Union Pacific and the Central Pacific build?

11. What did the pioneers use windmills for?

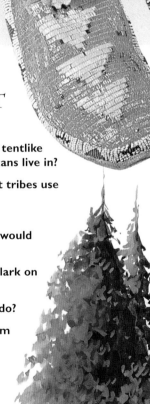

Quiz questions

THE CIVIL WAR

1. Which state had two presidents?

2. What was Harriet Tubman's nickname?

3. Which famous president was very tall?

4. Which side sang *Yankee Doodle*?

5. What was a pumpkin slinger?

6. What was an ironclad?

7. What were teeth dullers?

8. Who was nicknamed "Stonewall"?

9. Who won the Battle of Gettysburg?

10. Which woman helped in the hospitals?

11. Which was the most common medical operation carried out on Civil War soldiers?

12. In which year did slavery officially end?

PRESIDENTS

1. Where is the Oval Office?

2. What is the name of the president's plane?

3. Which president was a smart dresser?

4. How old was Ronald Reagan when he was inaugurated?

5. What does CIA stand for?

6. Which Olympics did Jimmy Carter order a boycott of?

7. Who did Lee Harvey Oswald shoot?

8. Who grew peanuts before becoming president?

9. What medal did John F. Kennedy win?

10. Which president received a dog as a present?

11. Where are the greatest American presidents' heads carved into rock?

SPORTING HEROES

1. What did Walter Camp invent?

2. Which sport has the Queensberry Rules?

3. What golfing championship started in 1898?

4. What was Gentleman Jim's real name?

5. Who was the first black professional footballer?

6. What was Helen Wills' nickname?

7. Who was married to Joe DiMaggio?

8. Who said "Float like a butterfly, sting like a bee"?

9. What is Jack Nicklaus' nickname?

10. Which tennis star was engaged to Chris Evert?

11. What nationality is Martina Navratilova?

GREAT AMERICANS

1. What is the nickname of the U.S. government?

2. Which Baptist clergyman led the civil rights movement in the 1960s?

3. Who is Billy Graham?

4. Who started Microsoft?

5. What year did U.S. astronauts first step onto the Moon?

6. What was William Frederick Cody's other name?

7. Who wrote *A Farewell to Arms*?

8. What instrument did Sachem play?

9. Which pop star was killed in a plane crash?

10. Who invented the telephone?

11. Who is Cassius Clay?

Index

A

Aaron, H. 208
Abdul-Jabbar, K. 209
abolitionists 130, 131, 135
Acoma 21, 99
Adams, A. 236
Adams, J. 158, 160, 178, 179, 181, 219
Adams, J.Q. 175, 181
Addams, J. 221
Afghanistan 169
Agnew, S. 160
Air Force One 159, 169
Alabama 143
Alabama 32
Alamo 21
Alaska 13, 57
Alcatraz 19
Alcindor, L. 209
Alcott, L.M. 153, 230
Aldrin, B. 227
Algonquian 50, 68, 73
Ali, M. 206, 209, 212, 214, 242
America River 112, 113
American Fur Company 107
American Indian Movement 65
Amos, R. 193
amputations 152
Anasazi 44
Anderson Prison 150, 151
Anne 84
Anson, C. 191
Anthony, S. 220
Antietam Creek 146, 147
Apache 41, 51, 55, 61, 62, 63, 100
Apalachee 51, 55
Appalachian Mountains 30, 99, 128
Appalachians 94, 95
Arabella 86
Arapaho 58
Arbor Day 22
Arizona 20, 21, 39, 44, 54, 61
Arkansas 30
Armstrong, L. 234
Armstrong, N.A. 227
Army Medical Museum 149
Arthur, C. 160
Ashe, A. 209
Astor, J.J. 224
Astor, N.W. 219
Attorney General 165
Audubon, J.J. 236

B

babies 50
back-woodsmen 95
Baldwin, J. 231
Balloon Corps 141
Bank of America 171
Barnard, E.E. 240
Barnum, P.T. 228
Barrow, R. 139
Barton, C. 152, 221
baseball 155, 189, 191—193, 195—198, 201—203, 205, 208, 214
Basie, W. 232
basketball 189, 193, 205, 209, 211—212
battles 146, 147, 148, 149, 151, 152
battleships 142
Bay of Pigs 169
bayonets 138
Beamon, B. 207
Belgium 175
Bell, A.G. 241
Berlin, I. 232
Bernstein, L. 232
Billy the Kid 20, 122
Birdseye, C. 224
Black Hills 125
Blackfeet 40, 58, 59
Blackwell, E. 239
Blaine, J. 179
blockades 143
Bogart, H. 229
Boone, D. 94, 95
Boonesborough 95
Booth, J.W. 154, 173
border ruffians 131
Boston 86
Boston Tea Party 27
Bouvier, J. 180
boxing 188—190, 193—194, 199—200, 204, 206, 209, 213
Boyd, B. 141
Braddock, J. 200
Bradford, D. 79
Bradford, W. 74, 77, 79, 85
Brady, M.B. 140
Brains Trust 179
Brando, M. 229
Brannan, S. 113
Brewster, W. 74, 75
Brezhnev, L. 164
bridges 140
Britain 143
broncos 120
Brooks, P. 131
Brown, J. 29, 130, 133, 134, 154, 207, 215, 220

Buchanan, J. 167
buffalo 40, 42, 43, 45, 47, 48, 49, 51, 55, 63, 99, 100, 105, 107, 117, 119, 124—5
Buffalo Calf Road Woman 59
Bull Run 146, 147
Bunker Hill 93
burial mounds 38
Burns, T. 194
Bush, G. 6, 169, 174, 176, 183
Buskirk, D. Van 137
Butler, General 138
Butler, N.M. 237
Byrd, R.E. 227
Babe Ruth 243

C

cabinets 165
Cabot, J. 70
Calamity Jane 13
California 17, 18, 57, 107, 110, 112—115, 117
Camp, W. 188
canoes 83, 89
Cape Cod 77, 78
Capra, F. 228
Carlson, C.F. 241
Carnegie, A. 221
carpetbaggers 155
Carson, K. 58, 107
Carter, J. 71, 164, 169, 175
Cartwright, A. 189, 191
Carver, J. 78, 79, 81
Cascade Mountains 10, 11, 98, 111
Cassidy, B. 122
casualties 152
Catlin, G. 62
cattle 120, 121
Central Intelligence Agency (CIA) 164
Central Pacific 116, 117
Chamberlain, W. 207
Champlain, S. de 71, 88
Cherokee 23, 29, 40, 47, 51, 55, 59, 60, 63, 64, 94
Chesapeake 71
Cheyenne 40, 58, 59
Chickasaws 23
Chicksaw 40, 50
Chief Joseph 59
Chief Looking Glass 60
children 74, 75, 119
China 117
Chinook 98, 99
Chippewa 40
Chirricahua 63
Chisholm Trail 120
Choctaw 23, 40, 42, 44, 47, 50, 51, 55

H

I

J

K

L